PLAYS BY

EDWARD ALBEE

EVERYTHING
IN THE
GARDEN

EDWARD ALBEE'S

EVERYTHING IN THE GARDEN

FROM THE PLAY BY GILES COOPER

NEW YORK 1968

ATHENEUM

Copyright © 1968 by Edward Albee
From the play Everything in the Garden *by Giles Cooper,*
copyright © 1963, 1964 by Giles Cooper
All rights reserved
Library of Congress catalog card number 68–16862
Published simultaneously in Canada by McClelland and Stewart Ltd.
Manufactured in the United States of America by H. Wolff, New York
Designed by Harry Ford
First Edition

TO THE MEMORY OF

GILES COOPER

1435331

FIRST PERFORMANCE

November 16, 1967, New York City, Plymouth Theatre

BARBARA BEL GEDDES *as* JENNY

BARRY NELSON *as* RICHARD

ROBERT MOORE *as* JACK

BEATRICE STRAIGHT *as* MRS. TOOTHE

RICHARD THOMAS *as* ROGER

MARY K. WELLS *as* BERYL

WHITFIELD CONNOR *as* CHUCK

M'EL DOWD *as* LOUISE

TOM ALDREDGE *as* GILBERT

CHARLES BAXTER *as* PERRY

AUGUSTA DABNEY *as* CYNTHIA

Directed by PETER GLENVILLE

THE PLAYERS

RICHARD
a pleasant-looking man, 43

JENNY
his wife, an attractive woman in her late thirties

ROGER
their son, a nice-looking boy, 14 or 15

JACK
a neighbor, a pleasant-looking man, about 40

MRS. TOOTHE
an elegantly dressed, handsome lady, 50 or so

CHUCK AND BERYL

GILBERT AND LOUISE

CYNTHIA AND PERRY
friends and neighbors,
very much like Richard and Jenny

THE SCENE

The livingroom and sunroom of a suburban house, a large and well-kept garden visible through the glass doors of the sunroom. This was an old house and the sunroom is clearly an addition to the existing structure, though not jarring. There is no wealth evident in the set; taste and ingenuity have been used instead of money.

ACT ONE

SCENE ONE

(Stage empty, sounds of lawnmower (hand) out picture window. RICHARD *passes window, mowing; stops, mops; goes on.* JENNY *enters room from hall, looking for a cigarette; finds pack on mantel, finds it empty, is about to throw it away, remembers, removes coupons, then is about to throw pack in wastebasket when she spies another empty pack therein, shakes her head, stoops, takes it out, un-crumples it, removes coupons)*

JENNY

(Shakes her head; under her breath)
Honestly! *(Louder, but* RICHARD *cannot possibly hear)* You might remember!
   *(*RICHARD *passes window again, mowing;* JENNY
   opens glass door, speaks out to him)*
You might remember!
     (He goes on mowing; irritated)
Richard!
     (He stops)

RICHARD

(We really don't hear him)

Hm?

JENNY

You might try to remember! *(Turns, comes back in, leaving glass door open)*

RICHARD

(Follows her in, mopping neck with handkerchief)
I might what?

JENNY

You might remember. *(Leaves it at that)*

RICHARD

(Thinks)

All right. *(Pause)* I might remember what?

JENNY

(Still looking for a cigarette)

When you throw them away.

RICHARD

(Considers that)

Um-hum. *(Pause)* May I go back out now? *Somebody's* got to get the damn lawn mowed, and I don't notice any gardeners out there waiting for me to tell them what . . .

JENNY

(Finding every cigarette box empty)

I've told you two thousand times: well, I've told you *two* things two thousand times: please keep cigarettes in the house . . .

RICHARD

(Used to it, but airy)

You're running it.

JENNY

(Something of the strict schoolteacher creeping in)

When you finish a pack, do two things—I've told you . . .

RICHARD

—two thousand times—

JENNY

(Closes her eyes for a moment, goes on)

. . . first, when you finish a pack, look to see if it's the last one—the last pack . . .

RICHARD
(Bored, impatient)

Yes, ma'am.

JENNY
(Undaunted)

And if it is, put it down to get some more, or tell *me* . . .

RICHARD
(Ibid.)

O.K.; O.K.

JENNY

Whenever you *do* finish a pack, don't forget to take the coupons off. Please? The coupons? We save them?

RICHARD

Did I *forget*?

JENNY

You *always* forget. We smoke these awful things just to get the coupons . . .

RICHARD
(Offhand)

O.K.

JENNY
(After a small pause)

Do you have any?

RICHARD

Coupons?

JENNY
(Not amused)

Cigarettes!

RICHARD
(Feels)
Um-hum. *(Suddenly aware)* Want one? *(Offers her the pack)*

JENNY
(Sees the pack)
Why, you dog! Those aren't . . . What are you—how dare
you smoke *those* cigarettes, those don't have coupons,
you . . . Do you mean I sit in here, ruining my lungs, piling
up coupons, while you're sneaking around . . .

RICHARD
(Giggles at being caught)
Caught me, huh?

JENNY
You little . . . twerp!

RICHARD
(Lighting for her)
Big twerp. Good, aren't they?

JENNY
(Rue)
Yes. *(Pause)* How's the lawn?

RICHARD
Growing.

JENNY
Remember what I told you: watch out for the tulips.

RICHARD
(Exaggerated contrition)
Well, I gotta confess I got carried away, zooming along with
the mower, *(Fast shiver sound)* br-br-br-br-br-br-br-br, mowed

'em down; by the time I got control of myself must have chopped up a good two dozen of 'em. *(Afterthought)* Sorry.

JENNY
(Nods knowingly)
Well, it wasn't funny that time you did. *(More-or-less to herself)* Honestly, a grown man running a lawnmower through a tulip bed.

RICHARD
(Jaunty and proud)
I rather liked it. Besides, what do you mean, "How's the lawn?" What do you care about the lawn? It could turn into one big dandelion patch for all you'd care so long as it didn't interfere with your hollyhocks and your tulips and your pink Williams, or whatever they are.

JENNY
(Superior, but friendly)
We all do what we're equipped for. Some of us are fit for keeping a lawn cut, and others . . . well, how green is my thumb.

RICHARD
(Looks at it all)
Looks good. Your scrambled eggs are a mess, but you sure can keep a garden.

JENNY
(Sweet-and-sour)
I'm just an outdoor type.

RICHARD
(Kisses her forehead)
Yes. You are. *(Collapses in an easy chair; groans with fatigue)*
OOOOOHHHHhhhhhhhhhhhh, God!

JENNY

Hm?

RICHARD
(Sincere and sad)

I *wish* we could afford things.

JENNY
(Muted; ironic)

Keep smoking! Save those coupons!

RICHARD

Roger call? He get to school O.K.?

JENNY

Yes, he has three roommates this year, and they're going to let him have his bike.

RICHARD
(Very young again)

I wish they'd let me have a power mower.

JENNY

Well, you can't have one, so just . . . (Leaves it unfinished)

RICHARD

I am probably the only natural-born citizen east of the Rockies who does not have a power mower.

JENNY

Well, you cannot *have* one, so let it be.

RICHARD
(Points vaguely around, suggesting the neighborhood)

Alan has one; Clinton; *Mark!* Mark's got one he trades *in* every . . .

JENNY
(*Surprisingly sharp*)

No!

(*Silence*)

RICHARD
(*To himself*)
Forty-three years old and I haven't even got a power mower.
(*Silence*)

JENNY

Do you want something? Some tea, or a sandwich?

RICHARD
(*Sharp*)

Can we afford it?

JENNY
(*Through her teeth*)

Barely.

RICHARD
(*Gets up, paces; offhand*)
You, uh . . . you want to get a divorce? Get married again?
Somebody with money? Somebody with a power mower?

JENNY
(*Weary, matter-of-fact*)
Not this week; I'm too busy.

RICHARD
(*Abstracted*)
You let me know. (*Back to her*) How much?

JENNY

Hm?

RICHARD

How much do you spend? On, on seeds, and manure, and shears, and . . .

JENNY
(Gets up)

Oh, for God's . . .

RICHARD

. . . and, and bulbs, and stakes to hold the damn plants up, and . . .

JENNY
(Angry, but, still, rather bravura)

Plow it up! Plow the whole damn garden under! Put in gravel! And while you're at it, get rid of the grass!

RICHARD
(Shrugs)

Everybody has grass.

JENNY
(Furious)

EVERYBODY HAS A GARDEN! *(Still angry, but softer)* I am willing; I am willing to scrimp, and eat what I don't really want to half the time, and dress like something out of a forties movie . . .

RICHARD
(Regretting the whole thing)

All right; all right . . .

JENNY

. . . and *not* have a maid, and only have my hair done twice a month, and not say let's go away for the weekend . . .

RICHARD

All right!

JENNY

. . . to pay and pay on this god-damned house . . .

RICHARD
(Soft, reasonable, but infuriating)
. . . everybody has a house . . .

JENNY

. . . *and* the bloody car . . .

RICHARD

. . . we need a car . . .

JENNY

. . . *and* Roger's school . . .

RICHARD
(Ire up a little)
When the public schools in this country . . .

JENNY

. . . *and* all the insurance . . .

RICHARD

We die, you know.

JENNY

. . . and everything else! Every money-eating thing!

RICHARD

Don't forget the government; *it's* hungry.

JENNY

I'll do it all, I'll . . . I'll smoke those awful cigarettes,
I'll . . . but I *will* not. I *will* not give up my garden.

RICHARD
(Gentle: placating)
I wouldn't *ask* you to.

JENNY
We live beyond our means, we have no right to be here,
we're so far in the hole you'll have to rob a bank or something, we've . . .

RICHARD
I love your garden.

JENNY
(Quieting down some)
There are some things I will just not do: and first in line is
I will not give up my garden.

RICHARD
No; of course not.

JENNY
I *love* my garden.

RICHARD
Y*es.*

JENNY
The way the florist charges, if we had to buy *cut* flowers . . .

RICHARD
I *know;* I *know.*

JENNY
Now, if we had a greenhouse . . .

RICHARD
A greenhouse!

JENNY

Yes, well, a small one, just enough to raise some orchids
in . . .

> *(Sees* RICHARD *rise, move off shaking his head)*

. . . Where are you going?

RICHARD

I'm going out to kill myself.

JENNY

But why!?

RICHARD
> *(Losing control)*

Do you know how much a greenhouse costs!?

JENNY
> *(Getting mad)*

I'M TRYING TO SAVE MONEY!

RICHARD
> *(Dismissing her)*

You're insane.

JENNY

Do you *know* how much cut flowers *cost*?

RICHARD
> *(Mimicking her)*

Do you *know* how much a greenhouse *costs*?

JENNY

I am *trying* to save *money.*

RICHARD
> *(Tiny pause, then)*

Then why don't you go to Paris and buy Christian Dior!?
That way you won't have to pay for your dresses.
> *(Silence)*

JENNY
(Preoccupied)
Do you want some tea? Or a sandwich?
(RICHARD *shakes his head; silence*)
(*A little sad, wistful, but reassuring*)
We will have a greenhouse, someday. I'll make it nice; you'll
have a livingroom full of flowering plants; you'll like it very
much.

RICHARD
(Mildly ironic, sad)
Can I have a power mower first?

JENNY
(Nice)
You can have *every*thing.

RICHARD
(Sighs)
That will be nice.

JENNY
(Wistful)
And so can I, and everything will be lovely.

RICHARD
(After a silence)
The thing I don't like about being poor . . .

JENNY
(Correcting by rote)
. . . about not having money . . .

RICHARD
The thing I don't like about being—about not having
money . . .

JENNY
(*A little embarrassed, as if someone might overhear*)
We're not *starving*.

RICHARD
No, we eat, but if we didn't belong to the, the (*Points out the window*) club we'd eat a lot better.

JENNY
(*Patient agreement*)
Yes.

RICHARD
If we didn't try to live like our friends we might put something away sometime.

JENNY
(*Ibid.*)
Um-hum.

RICHARD
Friends we didn't have, by the way, until we moved here, took this place . . .

JENNY
But *friends*.

RICHARD
Oh, yeah, well, you find them. (*Tossed-off, but sincere*) We don't live right.

JENNY
(*Throws her head back, laughs*)
Oh God!

RICHARD
We don't!

JENNY

Poor baby.

RICHARD
(As if in a debate)
You live in a forty-thousand-dollar house and you have to
smoke bad cigarettes to get the coupons so you can afford a
good vacuum so you can clean it; you belong to the club so
you can pay back dinner invitations from people you
wouldn't even know if you hadn't joined the club in the first
place, and you *joined* the club, *and* learned how to play tennis, because you decided to move into a neighborhood where
everybody belonged to the club.

JENNY
(Noncommittal)
Except the Jews and the tradespeople.

RICHARD
Hm? You're up to hock in your eyebrows . . . (Realizes
what he has said, tries to fix it, retaining dignity) . . . up in
hock to your . . . in hock up to your eyebrows, and why!

JENNY
(Calm, nonplussed)
Because you want to live nicely.

RICHARD
I do?

JENNY
(Eyes closed briefly in martyrdom)
Because *we* do, because we want to live nicely; because we
want to live the way a lot of people manage . . .

RICHARD
Yes; people who can afford it!

JENNY

No! The way a lot of other people *cannot* afford it, and still
do. Do you think the mortgage department of the bank stays
open just for us?

RICHARD

Look at Jack!

JENNY

Jack is rich! Look at everybody else.

RICHARD
(Pause; glum)

I don't feel I belong anywhere.

JENNY
(Slightly patronizing commiseration)

Awww; poor Richard.

RICHARD

It *does*, by the way.

JENNY
(Very straightforward, even a little suspicious)

What does what?

RICHARD

The bank; the mortgage department; stays open just for us.

JENNY
(Laughs a little)

You don't want a sandwich, or something?

RICHARD
(Preoccupied)

No.

JENNY
(Clear they've had this before)
I'm still able-bodied . . .

RICHARD
(Firm)
No.

JENNY
Lots of wives do it.

RICHARD
No.

JENNY
Just part-time, only from . . .

RICHARD
You may *not* get a job!

JENNY
It would make all the difference in . . .

RICHARD
(Out of patience, now)
No, now! *(Softer afterthought)* I'm not going to have a wife
of mine trying to work at some job, *and* running a house, *and*
looking after Roger when he's home from school . . .

JENNY
Roger is fourteen, he doesn't need any looking after.

RICHARD
No! Besides, he's fifteen.

JENNY
And if I *took* a job, then we could afford a maid, and . . .

RICHARD

I said *no.*

JENNY
(*Exasperated*)
Well, it wouldn't be taking in laundry, for God's sake!

RICHARD
(*Slightly nasty*)
No? What would it be?

JENNY
(*She, too*)
Well, that may be all you think I'm good for . . .

RICHARD
(*Voice rising*)
I didn't *say* that.

JENNY

Well, you *inferred* it!

RICHARD
Implied; not inferred. And I did not.

JENNY
Yes you did, for God's sake.

RICHARD
I said nothing of the sort.

JENNY
(*Snotty, exaggerated imitation*)
No? Well, what would it *be*? What could you do? (*Anger*)
Is that all you think I'm good for?

RICHARD
(Trying patience now)
I didn't say that all you could do was take in laundry; I
merely meant that . . .

JENNY
(Starting to cry)
I'm sorry you think so badly of me.

RICHARD
(Eyes to heaven)
Oh, for Christ's . . .

JENNY
(Sniffling; the whole act which is not an act)
I'm sorry you think that's all I'm good for. I *try* to help you;
I try to run a decent house . . .

RICHARD
It's a *lovely* house . . .

JENNY
. . . and bring up your son so he won't be some . . . some
ruffian . . .

RICHARD
. . . *our* son . . .

JENNY
I try to *look* nice; I try to take care of myself, for *you*, for
your friends . . .

RICHARD
What, what is this everything *mine* all of a sudden! Most of
the time it's yours; all yours!

JENNY
(Real tears again)

I try! I try!

RICHARD

Oh, Lord! *(Comes over, comforts her)* You do a *lovely* job; you run everything just . . . lovely; you look . . . you look good enough to eat. *(Snarls, tries to bite her neck)*

JENNY
(Martyr)

Don't, now.

(RICHARD repeats snarl, bite)

Just don't!

(RICHARD moves away)

Just . . . just go away.

RICHARD
(Pause; subdued)

I didn't mean to . . . say anything to upset you.

JENNY

No, but you *meant* it!

RICHARD
(Anger rising)

I did not *mean* it!

JENNY
(Angry, too)

Then why did you *say* it!!?

RICHARD
(Eyes narrowed)

What?

JENNY
(Cold)
If you didn't mean it, then why did you say it?

RICHARD
I didn't say what . . . you implied that I . . .

JENNY
Inferred!

RICHARD
SKIP IT!
(Silence)

JENNY
(Great soft-spoken dignity)
I was merely trying to suggest that I might be able to help
at the hospital one or two afternoons a week . . .

RICHARD
(Snorts)
And make enough to pay a maid out of that?

JENNY
(Trying to stay calm)
Or open a hat shop . . .

RICHARD
You're mad! You're absolutely mad!

JENNY
(Very sincere plea)
I just want to help?
(Silence)

RICHARD
(With her again; nicely)
I know you do. And you do as much as anyone; you do more
than your share.

JENNY

No, no, I don't do *anything* to help you.

RICHARD
(Nuzzles)

You do *every*thing.

JENNY

You think I'm worthless.

RICHARD
(To make light of it)

No, I imagine I could sell you for about . . . oh . . .

JENNY
(Won't go along)

You think I'm a drag; I'm not a helpmeet. Lots of women have part-time jobs, just to help out, it . . .

RICHARD
(Final)

No!

JENNY
(After a silence; sighs)

Money, money, money.

RICHARD

That's how it's always been. That's how it *is*.

JENNY
(Comforting)

You earn more than you used to.

RICHARD

Earn: yes. Taxes. Beware the steady man! Beware the slow rise through the respectable ranks.

(JACK *appears in the french doors, enters, observes,*
lolls, speaks to the audience; becomes a part of the
action only when he speaks directly to one or
another of the characters)

JENNY

I know; Mother told me I should marry a real-estate specu-
lator.

RICHARD
(*Going to the liquor cupboard*)
Yes; well, well you should.

JENNY
(*One more try*)
So, if I had just a *little* job . . .

RICHARD
(*Looking among bottles*)

No!

JACK
(*To the audience, while* RICHARD *hunts among the*
bottles)
Are they arguing about money? Poor things; they always do.
They're very nice, though. Richard is decent, and Jenny is
. . . good. Damn it; wish she weren't.

JENNY
(*Unaware of* JACK)
What are you looking for?

RICHARD
(*Ibid., not looking up from the bottles*)
The vodka.

JENNY
There's some right there; right there in front of you.

RICHARD

Not *my* kind; not the Polish, only party stuff—American.

JENNY
("Get you")

Oh; well, sorry.

RICHARD

It's empty anyway.

JACK
(To the audience)

You see? That's it. The Polish vod is eight bucks a fifth. That's what makes the difference: taste; and taste is expensive. Poor children. *(A confidence)* I find Jenny *so attractive.* Not that I'm going to jump her, or anything. My letch is in the mind; *is; generally.*

RICHARD
(To JENNY*)*

Decent vodka is not a luxury.

JENNY

Nor is a greenhouse.

RICHARD

Yes it is.

JACK
(To the audience)

My uncle died and left *me* three-and-a-quarter mill. Which is very nice. Which means *I* can have a greenhouse, *and* the Polish vodka, *plus* the thirty-year scotch, plus . . . never worry—which is the nicest of all, don't you think? *(In the action now)* Hello, children!

RICHARD

Hm?

JENNY
(Piqued and pleased, her reaction to JACK *is always
a combination of maternal and coquettish)*
Oh, for God's sake, Jack!

RICHARD
(His reaction to JACK *is a combination of slight mis-
trust, discomfort, and natural friendliness)*
Well, hello there, Jack.

JACK
(Sees they are a little embarrassed)
Ah, when I am wandering, footsore and loose, where do I
always come? *Here.* And why? Well, for a warm and toasty
welcome. How are you, children?

RICHARD
Poor.

JENNY
Fine!

JACK
Don't go together.

RICHARD
How've you been?

JACK
(Kisses JENNY *on the forehead)*
Stopped by the club to watch the heart attacks, looked in on
the poker game and dropped a couple of hundred. *(To*
JENNY*)* You . . . smell . . . lovely.

JENNY
(Pleased)
Thank you.

JACK

And . . . thought I'd come over the fence and see you two.

RICHARD
(Nice, but an undertone)

I'll bet you'd like a drink.

JENNY
(To cover)

Ummm; me too!

JACK

Love one. Polish vod?

RICHARD
(A look at JENNY*)*

Fresh out.

JENNY
(To RICHARD*)*

Why don't you make us all a nice martini?

JACK
(Clucks; false disapproval)

Drink drink drink.

RICHARD

No vermouth either.

JACK

Such hospitality; I *tell* you.

RICHARD

I'll go get some.

JACK

Perfect! That way I get to be alone with your wife.

JENNY

Oh, Jack!

RICHARD
(To suggest, "If you are, I'll go get some")
You staying long?

JENNY
(Cheerful admonition)

Richard!

JACK

Well, what I thought I'd do is have one final drink with the two of you. You see, I've settled a quarter of a million on each of you, and after I had my drink I thought I'd go down in the cellar and kill myself.

JENNY

Awwwwww.

RICHARD
(A little grim)
You ought to do it somewhere else; we might have trouble getting the money if . . . *(Leaves it unfinished)*

JENNY
(Playing the game)
Yes . . . they might . . . *you* know . . . ask questions.

JACK
(To the audience)
He's right there, you know. Good mind. *(Back into action)* Oh. *(Pause)* Do you think? Yes; well, all right. I'll just have the drink, then.

RICHARD
(Slight, uncertain pause)
O.K. *(Pause)* Well, I'll go get some.

JACK

Go, bucko; go.

JENNY
(Giggles)
Oh, honestly, Richard; I'll be all right.

JACK
You have a faithful wife, Richard; never fear. *(To the audience)* He has, too. She's rare; she's a good woman.

RICHARD
(Moving to exit, through hallway)
I know; it's the only kind I ever marry.

JACK
(Genuine surprise)
You been married before?

RICHARD
(Surprise)
No. I was just . . . *(At a loss for words)* . . . it was just a . . . something to say. *(To* JENNY*)* You, you want anything? At the store?

JENNY
(Shakes her head)
Unh-unh. Hurry back. Oh! Cigarettes!

RICHARD
(About to exit; a little bitter)
Which kind?

JENNY
(A giving-up sigh and smile)
The ones we like. Hurry, now.
                    (RICHARD *exits)*

JACK
(To the departed RICHARD*)*
By-ee! *(To* JENNY, *almost Groucho Marx)* Quick! He'll be
fifteen minutes even at a dog trot! Where's the guestroom?

JENNY
(Laughs)
Oh, come on, Jack! Besides, you aren't even a guest.

JACK
(Seemingly surprised)
No? What am I?

JENNY
A . . . uh . . . a fixture.

JACK
Something from the neighborhood? Bothersome Jack, here-
he-comes-again-probably-drunk-and-time-on-his-hands-so-why-
not-waste-everybody-else's-afternoon-while-he's-at-it?

JENNY
Mnnnnn.

JACK
(To the audience)
Am, too. Like that, I mean. Time, time. God, the ambition
you have to have to overcome good fortune. I haven't *got* it.
(Back to JENNY*) Let* me paint your picture.

JENNY
(Cheerful, but it's clear they've had this before)
No.

JACK
Won't cost you a penny.

JENNY

No.

JACK
(To the audience)
I'm not a bad painter. Flattering portraits of the rich? *(Back to* JENNY*)* What is it, then?

JENNY

I . . . just want to be different.

JACK
(Mild lechery)
Oh, you *are*, Jenny.

JENNY

Every, every house I go into, every time Richard and I go out, there it is! Sybil, Grace Donovan, Junie, Mrs. what's-her-name, Beachcomber, or something; *over* the mantel, badly framed, the lady of the house; your portrait.

JACK
(Axiom)
Ladies *like* to be painted, *I* paint ladies, ladies hang pictures.

JENNY
(Apologetic)
It isn't proper.

JACK
(Brief laugh)
Tell 'em in Newport; put me out of business. *(Digging)* Besides, I bet I make more money in three good months up there than Richard does in a whole . . .

JENNY

Oh, *money!*

JACK
(Waits a moment; quietly, smiling)
Yes? Money?

JENNY
I just don't . . . I don't want to look at myself, that's all.

JACK
(Very elegant)
If I were you . . . I would. *(Normal tone)* What's the matter, love?

JENNY
Oh . . . *(Very sincere, even plaintive, for a joke)* Would you do it, Jack? Go down in the cellar? I mean, leave Richard and me a quarter of a million each and then go kill yourself somewhere? I mean that nicely.

JACK
I'd do almost anything for you. *(Afterthought, but not flip)* Unless it got in the way of what I wanted to do for me. *(JENNY laughs ruefully)* What is it, puss?

JENNY
(Not going to talk about it)
Tired. Just . . . tired.

JACK
Want a shoulder to cry on?

JENNY
Nope; just a quarter of a million and an easy mind.

JACK
(Shakes his head knowingly)
Wouldn't help. Money's hungry, lonely, wants more of itself. Stay poor; you're better off.

JENNY
(Snorts)
Crap!

(The doorbell rings; JENNY *goes toward the hallway)*

JACK
Really; you are.

JENNY
(Going)
You'd *know*.

JACK
I *watch*. (JENNY *has gone;* JACK *addresses the audience)* I
have; it *does*; money always wants more to keep it company.
And a little money is a dangerous thing. Don't aim for a
million: that's the danger point. If I were to *die* . . . I
wouldn't leave them a quarter of a million each. Bad. I'd
leave 'em the whole damn three. As a matter of fact, that
isn't a bad idea at all. With three mill plus, they wouldn't
have to worry. I think I'll do it. Yes; consider it done. *(Con-*
siders) I am *healthy*, though. They might not get it till it's
way too late. Still . . . consider it done.

JENNY'S VOICE
(From the hallway)
No, of course not, don't be silly.

(JENNY appears, followed by MRS. TOOTHE)

MRS. TOOTHE
(Entering)
I *should* have phoned before just appearing at your door, but
I thought that on . . . Ah, this must be your husband. How
do you do, I'm Mrs. Toothe, and your wife has been kind
enough to . . .

JENNY
(A *little laugh*)
Oh, no, this isn't Richard—my husband, I mean . . .

MRS. TOOTHE
Ah. Well.

JENNY
(A *little lame*)
This is just . . . Jack.

MRS. TOOTHE
(*Extends her hand to* JACK)
No matter. How do you do, just the same.

JACK
(*Takes hand, does curt little formal bow*)
Mrs. Toothe.

JENNY
(*Lame, and embarrassed by it*)
Jack was just . . . passing by.

MRS. TOOTHE
(*Noncommittal*)
A friend of the family; of course.

JENNY
Yes.

JACK
(*To* MRS. TOOTHE)
Not at all: a secret admirer of lovely Jenny. I only come
round when Richard's out. We have a signal—panties on the
laundry line.

JENNY
Jack!

MRS. TOOTHE

How divine!

JENNY
(*To* MRS. TOOTHE; *embarrassed and furious at being*)
There isn't a word of truth to what he says. There isn't a
word of truth to *any*thing he says, *ever*.

JACK
(*Still to* MRS. TOOTHE)
White panties if we've got one hour, yellow if we'll have to
hurry, pink for those special occasions . . .

JENNY
Jack! Please!

1435331

JACK
(*Shakes his head, sadly*)
I must confess it, madam, I am only what she says: a friend
of the family . . . dropping by. Damned attractive, though.
Wish it were true.

MRS. TOOTHE
(*Pleased and sympathetic*)
Ahhhh.

JENNY
Why is everybody standing? Please sit down, Mrs. . . .
uh . . . Toothe.

MRS. TOOTHE
(*Sits*)
Thank you.

JENNY
Jack, don't you think you should be . . . ?

JACK
(Makes it obvious he has gotten the signal)
By gum, I must be moving on! Different lines, more panties.
There is no rest for the wicked in the suburbs. Mrs. Toothe,
it's been . . .

MRS. TOOTHE
A great pleasure. And don't get your signals mixed.
      (JENNY accompanies JACK to the doors to the garden)

JACK
Tell Richard I'll be back for that martini another day. *(Sotto
voce)* Who is she, your fairy godmother?

JENNY
Will you go?

JACK
(Pecks her on the forehead)
Bye. *(To the audience, a wave before quick exit)* Bye.
      (JACK has gone; JENNY returns to MRS. TOOTHE)

JENNY
You mustn't believe a thing Jack says, Mrs. . . .

MRS. TOOTHE
(A hand up to silence her)
Oh, really. I can tell a lover from a friend.

JENNY
(Maybe even a little offended)
Oh? How?

MRS. TOOTHE
(Laughs)
Because in this country they're very seldom the same.

JENNY

You're English.

MRS. TOOTHE

Yes. Very.

(*Small silence*)

JENNY

Would you like some tea . . . or a drink?

MRS. TOOTHE
(*Very efficient*)

No thank you; this is business. Strictly business.

JENNY
(*Pause*)

Oh?

MRS. TOOTHE

I'm told you need a job?

JENNY
(*Somewhat confused*)

Who, who told you that?

MRS. TOOTHE
(*Airy*)

Oh, one of your friends. A woman.

JENNY
(*Curious, still puzzled*)

Oh? Who?

MRS. TOOTHE

No matter. Am I mistaken?

JENNY
(A *little ill-at-ease*)
Well, no . . . that is, I *was* thinking about getting a job . . .

MRS. TOOTHE
Yes, well, I thought so.

JENNY
Not a . . . a career, you understand, just something . . .

MRS. TOOTHE
. . . part *time*, something to bring a little extra money in.

JENNY
Well, yes; you know how it is: my son's away at school, and
I have the spare time. Besides, one can always use money,
can't one?

MRS. TOOTHE
(*Looking about, noncommittally*)
Yes; one can.

JENNY
These days, with taxes, and the private school . . .

MRS. TOOTHE
Oh, yes; yes; quite. What does your husband do?

JENNY
(*Uncomfortable, as if being interviewed*)
Well, he . . . he's a research chemist, and . . .

MRS. TOOTHE
. . . and that, as so many good things, pays less than it
should.

JENNY
(*Protecting* RICHARD)
Well, he doesn't do *too* badly; I mean . . .

MRS. TOOTHE
(The laugh again)
Of course not! But, still; you would like a job.

JENNY
*(Looks to the hallway, guilty—*RICHARD *might come back)*
Well, yes; one . . . one likes to feel useful.

MRS. TOOTHE
(Looking into her handbag)
Yes; useful. *(She takes out a thick bundle of bills, shows them to* JENNY) Money. (JENNY *just looks at it, her mouth falling open a little)* For you. *(Makes to give it to her)*

JENNY
Yes, but . . . *(Laughs a little, astounded)*

MRS. TOOTHE
(Nods her head)
Yes, money. For *you.* A thousand dollars. Here, take it.

JENNY
(Withdrawing a little from it)
Well, no, I . . .

MRS. TOOTHE
Count it if you like. Here; a thousand dollars. *(Tries to force it on her)*

JENNY
(A little panicked)
No!

MRS. TOOTHE
Very well. *(As calm as can be; rises, goes with the money to the fireplace, throws it on the burning logs)*

JENNY
*(Reflex, runs to the fireplace, almost puts her hands
into the fire, makes a little yell; straightens up, holds
on)*
Oh—I think you'd better go, Mrs. Toothe.

MRS. TOOTHE
(Enigmatic smile)
Not yet. Let's begin again. *(She takes another bundle of
money from her handbag, makes as if to throw it in the fire;
JENNY holds out her hand; MRS. TOOTHE quietly hands her
the money, resumes her seat; JENNY stays standing)*

JENNY
(Never taking her eyes off MRS. TOOTHE)
You're quite mad.

MRS. TOOTHE
No. Very rich.

JENNY
(Looks at the money, almost weighs it)
Look, you . . . you can't just . . . *give* me money like this.
I can't just . . . take money from you.

MRS. TOOTHE
(A little laugh)
You have. It's yours. Isn't there something you'd like to buy?
For yourself, for . . . what is his name? . . . Richard?

JENNY
People can't just give people money. I want to work.

MRS. TOOTHE
Good then. That's an advance of salary. You can work for
me.

JENNY

But I haven't *said* I'd take a job at *all*. Richard is *very* much against it, and . . .

MRS. TOOTHE
(*Daring her to refuse*)
I was told you needed money.

JENNY

Yes, but Richard wouldn't approve of anything like this, and . . .

MRS. TOOTHE

Like what? (*Indicates the money*) Wouldn't he approve of *that?*

JENNY
(*Looks at the money in her hands*)
I'm sorry; I didn't mean to be rude, but it's all so vague, isn't it? And . . . and so unexpected.

MRS. TOOTHE
(*Shrugs*)
It's a job.

JENNY
(*Nervous laughter in her voice*)
Well, you'll have to tell me what it *is*. I mean, money isn't everything.

MRS. TOOTHE

No? What isn't money? Here we are; this house is money, that garden, that lovely garden, those clothes you're wearing, it's all *money*, isn't it?

JENNY

The job?

MRS. TOOTHE
What are your husband's hours?

JENNY
He leaves at eight and gets home from town at seven-thirty,
but . . .

MRS. TOOTHE
Very good. *You'll* come in town, four afternoons a week,
from one to five, say. You'll come to my address—lovely
street: psychiatrist's office, doctors . . .

JENNY
Is this a . . . uh . . . a receptionist's job?

MRS. TOOTHE
Receptionist?

JENNY
Making, making appointments, and so on?

MRS. TOOTHE
I make appointments. For *you.*

JENNY
(Tiny pause)
For me? Who with?

MRS. TOOTHE
Clients.

JENNY
(Innocent)
What *for?*

MRS. TOOTHE
For a hundred dollars.

JENNY

No, I mean . . . A hundred dollars?

MRS. TOOTHE

More, sometimes—if they're generous.

JENNY

But these clients . . . who are they?

MRS. TOOTHE

Some businessmen, some visitors. All gentlemen; all rich.

JENNY
(The knowledge is there but not admitted yet)
What . . . exactly . . . what exactly would I do . . . for
this money?
*(MRS. TOOTHE laughs lightly; JENNY's jaw drops with
the admission; pause)*
*(JENNY picks up the bundle of money, holds it out
to MRS. TOOTHE; even, hard)*
Get out of my house.
*(MRS. TOOTHE does nothing; JENNY drops the money
on the table)*
I'll call the police.

MRS. TOOTHE
(As calm as anything; a little superior)
Whatever for?

JENNY
(Quivering)
You know what for!

MRS. TOOTHE
(Smiles)
I've said nothing.

JENNY

You know what you've suggested!

MRS. TOOTHE
(Shrugs)

That you make money.

JENNY

THAT WAY!

MRS. TOOTHE

You have a friend who does.

JENNY

Who!

MRS. TOOTHE

Oh, no; we're very discreet.

JENNY
(Through her teeth)

I don't believe you, not a word! People around here wouldn't
do that sort of thing; you don't realize; you don't know what
we're like.

MRS. TOOTHE
(Unconcerned)

Have it your way.

JENNY

One of the tradespeople, maybe; you're thinking of someone
like that.

MRS. TOOTHE

I'm thinking of a friend of yours; a very nice woman with a
lovely house, who keeps it nicely—much more nicely than
this, by the way—a woman who has no more worries about
money, who is very happy. So could you be.

JENNY

You're a filthy woman! IT'S DISGUSTING!!

MRS. TOOTHE
(Very calm)
Nothing is disgusting, unless one is disgusted.

JENNY

YOU'RE EVIL!!

MRS. TOOTHE

Yes, yes . . .

JENNY

I'LL TELL THE POLICE!

MRS. TOOTHE
(Stands up, stretches a little)
Good. Then perhaps they'll arrest me.

JENNY

I hope they put you in prison!

MRS. TOOTHE

Yes, well, they probably will, and then I shall admit everything.

JENNY

Everything?

MRS. TOOTHE

Yes, how you approached me, and we discussed it, but the terms didn't suit you. The *money* wasn't enough.

JENNY

THAT'S NOT TRUE!

MRS. TOOTHE

Perhaps not. I think it would be believed, though. By enough
people.

JENNY

GET OUT OF HERE!

MRS. TOOTHE
(Takes a calling card from her handbag)
Here is my card; address; telephone; let me know what you
decide.

JENNY
(Change of tone; almost tearful)
Please? Please go?

MRS. TOOTHE

No police then; good. *(Sees* JENNY *will not take the card, puts
it down next to the bundle of money on the table)* Don't telephone me before ten, though, please. I *do* like my sleep.

JENNY

Please? Go?

MRS. TOOTHE
(Smiles)
I'll see myself out. It's been very nice to meet you. *(Looks one
final time at the garden)* What a lovely garden. Do you have
a greenhouse?
(Smiles, exits, leaving JENNY *standing in the center
of the room)*
*(*JENNY *looks after* MRS. TOOTHE *for a long moment,
not moving. Then she looks down at the table
whereon sit the bundle of money and* MRS. TOOTHE'S
*card. She picks up the card, reads it, moving her lips,
then, with a grimace, rips the card in half and, as if
she were carrying feces, takes it over to a wastebasket*

and drops it in. She comes back to the table, stares at the money, picks it up, looks at it with detached fascination; doesn't know quite what to do with it; finally, rather firmly, puts it in desk drawer, locks drawer, keeps key, starts toward french doors, looks back at locked drawer, goes, stands at french windows looking out)

RICHARD'S VOICE
(From the hallway)

Hell-oo-oo. *(He enters, with a paper bag of liquor)* Oh, there you are. And who the hell was *that* tripping down our path, that bit of old England? "How do you do?" she . . . Where the hell *is* he—Jack?

JENNY
(Sort of vacant)

Oh. Hi.

RICHARD
(Puts liquor down, starts taking bottles out of bag)

Well, who *was* she—your fairy godmother?

JENNY
(Some alarm)

My what?

RICHARD

The woman; the lady. Who was she?

JENNY
(Still preoccupied)

Oh. Mrs. Toothe.

RICHARD

Mrs. what?

JENNY

Toothe; Toothe.

RICHARD

You're kidding. Where's Jack?

JENNY

It's a perfectly proper English name. *(Pause)* I guess. Jack?
He *went.*

RICHARD

Figures. Send me out to buy up the liquor store and off he
goes.

JENNY

It was *your* idea to go.

RICHARD
(A little cross)

Who *was* she?

JENNY

Mrs. Toothe? *(Tosses it off)* Oh . . . committee; wants me
for the hospital.

RICHARD

Free? Or pay?

JENNY
(Pause; casual)

Pay.

RICHARD

No!

JENNY
(Pause; softly)

All right.

RICHARD
(Looks at the liquor)
Well, with all your rich guests gone, there's just us for drinks.
What do you want . . . a martini?

JENNY
(Very sincere)
Yes, I think that would be *nice*.

RICHARD
O.K. *(Starts to make one; the ice is already there)*
You know what Tom Palmer said the other day?

JENNY
(Preoccupied, and not exactly unpleasant, but not pleasant either)
No, I don't; I didn't see Tom Palmer the other day. What did
Tom Palmer say?

RICHARD
(Looks up at JENNY for a moment, quizzically, then back to his work)
He said Jack was at the club, at the bar . . . soused as
usual . . .

JENNY
Jack isn't always drunk.

RICHARD
(A little annoyance)
He's always drinking.

JENNY
(Dogmatic)
That does *not* make him *drunk*.

RICHARD
I am merely repeating what Tom Palmer said.

JENNY

Tom Palmer's an old woman.

RICHARD
(Quite annoyed)

I do *not* want to argue!

JENNY

All right! *(Contrite)* I'm sorry, darling. *(Pause)* You're a good, decent man and I love you.

RICHARD
(Grudging)

Well, you're a good, decent woman, and I love you, too. As a matter of fact, I shall give you a house-special martini to show you how *much* I love you.

JENNY

Oh, I would like that.
(She comes for her drink, takes it from him, they put arms around each other, move toward the sofa; he kisses her on top of her head)

RICHARD

I think you smell even nicer than Jack does.

JENNY
(Purring)

When have you smelled Jack?

RICHARD

Than *Jack* thinks you smell.

JENNY

Oh.
(RICHARD tries to nip her neck)
Ow! Now stop that; I'll spill my martini.
(They sit on the sofa, relax)

RICHARD
(A *little bitter*)
You want to know something really funny?

JENNY
I don't *think* so. What?

RICHARD
I was in the liquor store . . .

JENNY
That's a riot.

RICHARD
Hush. I was in the liquor store, and Grady, who owns it, do
you know what he told me?

JENNY
No; what?

RICHARD
He's getting a second car? Not trading one in; getting a
second car.

JENNY
So?

RICHARD
Guy who owns a crummy little liquor store can have two
cars? And we have to get by with . . .

JENNY
Did you bring the cigarettes back with you?

RICHARD
Hm? (*Gets them out*) Oh; yes; here.

JENNY
(Takes one; so does he; he lights them both)
I wonder which kills more people: liquor or cars?

RICHARD
Well, when you put them together it's pretty good. What's
for dinner?
(Pause)

JENNY
Let's go *out* for dinner.

RICHARD
Where?

JENNY
(Expansive)
Let's . . . let's go to Le Cavalier.

RICHARD
(Snorts)
You must be out of your mind.

JENNY
No! Let's!

RICHARD
It'll cost twenty-five dollars each. After a drink, the wine,
it'll cost twenty-five each!
(Pause)

JENNY
(Cautiously)
I've got some money.

RICHARD
(Half hearing)
Hm?

JENNY

I said, *I've* got some money.

RICHARD
(Vaguely interested)

How?

JENNY
(Very offhand)

Oh, I've . . . put a little aside out of household. I keep a
little bit each week.

RICHARD
(Mildly)

Well, I'll be damned.

JENNY

Come on; let's go out; it'll do us good. Let's go to Le Cavalier. Let's live it up.

RICHARD

Let's pretend we can afford it?

JENNY

Sure! Come on; it'll do us both good.

RICHARD

You ingenious thing. How much have you got?

JENNY

Oh . . . enough. Come on now.

RICHARD

You clever girl. *(Rises)* I'd better wash up. Really? You have
enough?

JENNY
(Rises)

Yes. Better put things away in the garden before you get
cleaned up.

RICHARD

Right. *(Moves to the french doors)* You very clever girl.
(Goes outside)
> *(JENNY sees he is out of sight; goes slowly to the
> desk, unlocks the drawer, takes out the bundle of
> money, strips off several bills, puts them on the
> table, hesitates a moment, as to reconsider, then
> puts the rest of the money back in the drawer, locks
> it again, keeps the key. Stands for a moment; looks
> at the wastebasket, lifts it onto the table, takes the
> two halves of MRS. TOOTHE's card out, fits them to-
> gether, looks at the card. RICHARD pokes his head
> inside; JENNY doesn't flinch or try to hide the card,
> knowing that RICHARD either can't see it or won't ask
> what it is)*

RICHARD

Jenny?

JENNY

Hm?

RICHARD
(Sort of wistful)

Darling? How much does a greenhouse cost? You know . . .
a little one?

JENNY

Why?

RICHARD

I just wondered.

JENNY
(Looks up)

Quite a bit.

RICHARD

I just wondered. *(Returns outside)*

JENNY
(Looks at the card again, shakes her head; some rue)

Quite a bit.

CURTAIN

SCENE TWO

(*Six months later; scene the same; early afternoon;* RICHARD *at the desk, paying bills; shakes his head occasionally, despair. Sound of front door opening, closing.* JENNY *comes in, with bundles*)

JENNY
(*Cheerful*)

Hello.

RICHARD
(*Glum*)

Hello.

JENNY

On Saturday you're supposed to rest; why aren't you out working in the garden?
(RICHARD *laughs glumly*)
Or, or just . . . lying around?

RICHARD
(*Wan smile*)

Paying bills.

JENNY

Oh. (*Puts bundles down*) It figures, doesn't it: I go to the store and I forget half of what I want.

RICHARD

Didn't you make a list?

JENNY

Of course; I *got* everything on the list; I just didn't remember to put everything *on* the list.

RICHARD

Like what?

JENNY

Like what? Like . . . like root beer, and extra milk, and stuff for cookies, and . . .

RICHARD

What for?

JENNY

We have a son. Right?

RICHARD
(Preoccupied)

Um-huh.

JENNY
(Pause)

He's coming *home* today!

RICHARD
(Puzzlement, pleasure)

Roger? Today? Coming home?

JENNY
(As if he were addled)

Yes. Vacation.

RICHARD

Well, I'll be damned.

JENNY

Mmmmmmm. And cornflakes and stuff, I suppose.

RICHARD

No camp this year.

JENNY

Hm?

RICHARD

No camp this year. For Roger. No camp. Can't afford it.

JENNY
(*Noncommittal; her mind on something else*)
Oh. Really?

RICHARD

Really.

JENNY
(*Making her list*)
Well, afford or not, I thought it'd be nice if he was around
here this summer. Get to know him.

RICHARD
(*Adamantly grousing*)
Well, nice or not . . . necessary.

JENNY

Help *you*, help *me* . . .

RICHARD

While you're at it, get some more envelopes.

JENNY

There *are* some.

RICHARD

No, just that . . . that paper thing goes around them.

JENNY
(*Notes it down*)
All right. He can help you in the garden.

RICHARD
Mmmm. Or maybe we can get him a magazine route.

JENNY
(*Mild disgust and indignation*)
Really!

RICHARD
Well, you're so keen for everybody to be working around
here . . .

JENNY
He's just a child!

RICHARD
He's probably going steady already—got some local girl up
at school—probably skips out at night, shacked up . . .

JENNY
(*Protesting, embarrassed*)
Richard!

RICHARD
Kids grow up early nowadays.

JENNY
Roger is fourteen years old!

RICHARD
Well, if everything's functioning properly, there's no reason
why he can't be getting laid, is there? Besides, he's fifteen.

JENNY
That's enough now.

RICHARD
Well, it's better that than lots of other things.

JENNY
ALL RIGHT!

(Silence)

RICHARD
(Shakes his head, finally, a little sadly, smiles)
I knew a girl once, when you and I were dating—not so as
to say set the alarm for seven, or anything like that, but . . .

JENNY
(A little stony)
Don't regale me.

RICHARD
No; really. And I wasn't in on the good times, 'cause I was
counting on *you* . . .
(JENNY snorts)
and you met her, I think, but I won't tell you who she was,
cause she still *is* . . . but she had the reputation as a proper
put-out . . .

JENNY
(Some bored annoyance)
Please, Richard.

RICHARD
No. *More* than proper: something of a dedicatee, guest bedrooms at parties, drawing blood, literally . . .

JENNY
Let the poor woman *alone*.

RICHARD
(Slight edge)
I'm not *touching* her. (Silence) I was planning, though, to
compare her to *you*.

JENNY
(Sarcastic)

Really.

RICHARD

To your ad*van*tage.

JENNY
(Dripping irony)

Oooohhhh.

RICHARD

Socially—by which I mean out of bed, which is a euphe-
mism for trash heaps and coal bins—you'd think she was the
Queen Mother. Staid? She practically used the royal We. So
proper; you'd never know.

JENNY
(Not nice)

And what does that have to do with me?

RICHARD

Oh. It came up when I said Roger was probably going steady.

JENNY

Getting laid is what you said.

RICHARD

Same difference.

JENNY

Tell *that* to the sociologists.

RICHARD

They know. And I said Roger was probably going steady **and**
you came on all funny and red and . . .

JENNY

I didn't see any need for you to shout the house down,
and . . .

RICHARD
(Angry)

Who's going to hear? The footmen?

JENNY

Don't you yell at me!

RICHARD
(Pause; shake of head; laugh-whimper)

All I wanted to do was say you're such a funny, silly, wonderful little . . .

JENNY

Nuts.

RICHARD

You are! You're a good wife and you're nice in bed, but
you're funny and . . . prim.

JENNY

Prim!?

RICHARD

Yes! Prim!

JENNY

I'm *sorry*.

RICHARD

And then I thought about, uh, what's-her-name, who came
on like the Queen Mother, and how she was ridiculous and
you were just a little silly about it, and . . . *(Mumbles)* aw,
for Christ's sake, forget it. *(Pause)* I was just trying to pay
you a *comp*liment! I was *try*ing to be *nice*!

JENNY
(Thinks about it, dismisses his reasoning)
I don't see why you brought her up in the *first* place.

RICHARD
(Frustrated anger)
NEITHER DO I!

(Silence)

JENNY
I suppose I could learn a few dirty jokes, or start telling
people about a couple of your peculiarities when it comes
to . . .

RICHARD
Forget it!

(Silence)

JENNY
(Trying to hold back a smile)
Who was she?
(RICHARD *pouts, shakes his head)*
Come on; who was she?

RICHARD
No, no.

JENNY
(Tickles him a little)
Oh, come on!

RICHARD
(Happier)
No; now, stop it.
*(She tickles more, he grabs her, they wrestle, gig-
gling, a little on the sofa, playing, ending in a kiss,
then another, which prolongs, is far more serious)*

JENNY

Unh-unh; not now.

RICHARD

Ooooohhhh . . .

JENNY

No; Roger'll come in, and . . .

RICHARD

Well, he'll be able to tell his friends we're still alive.

JENNY

Now, come *on. No.*

RICHARD
(Leans back; sighs)

All right.

JENNY
(Pause)

Who was she?

RICHARD
(Shakes his head)

Unh-unh. I promised.

JENNY
(Eyes narrowing)

Who?

RICHARD

Myself. Self-discipline.

JENNY
(Disentangling)

Oh, honestly!

RICHARD

Well, a little doesn't hurt.

JENNY

(*Looking at herself in the mirror, appraisingly, approvingly*)

Did you see the paper today?

RICHARD

(*Preoccupied*)

Mmmmm.

JENNY

They had an ad.

RICHARD

(*Back to the desk*)

What are they doing, giving away money? I can sure use some, if they . . .

JENNY

(*Still appraising*)

No, for a greenhouse, all-aluminum frame, curved glass . . .

RICHARD

(*Slams a sheet of paper down*)

For Christ's sake, Jenny!

(*Pause, as she looks at him, a little haughtily*)

I just finished telling you Roger isn't going to camp this year because we can't afford it, and . . .

JENNY

(*Slight airy contempt*)

Oh, money-money-money.

RICHARD

Yes. Money. (*Shows bills*) Oil. The car. Con Ed—the bastards. An estimate on the attic—the leak.

(*Doorbell rings*)

JENNY

Doorbell.

RICHARD
(Back to work)
Yes. Why don't you get it?

JENNY
(Tiny pause)
Why don't you?

RICHARD

Hm?

JENNY

Why don't *you* get it?

RICHARD
(Slight whine)
Because I'm working, darling; can't you see I'm . . .

JENNY

What if it's for you?

RICHARD
(Slight bewilderment)
Then you can tell me who it *is*. Or *what*.

JENNY
(Pause, hesitation)
Oh. Yes, that's true.
(Doorbell again)

RICHARD
(Throws pen down, gets up, goes out)
Oh, for God's sake!
(Maybe, offstage, we hear RICHARD *saying "Yes?"*

and then "Oh, O.K." While he is offstage JENNY
moves about the room a little, practicing unconcern.
RICHARD *re-enters, with a small package: brown
paper, wrapped with twine, lots of stamps, special
delivery, etc.)*

JENNY

Who was it?

RICHARD
*(Looking at package, with some curiosity and dis-
taste)*
Package.

JENNY

Oh, for me?

RICHARD
No. For me. *(Shakes it, looks at it again)*

JENNY
(Pause)
Well. *(Pause)* Open it.

RICHARD
*(Putting it down on the table, stares at it, hands on
hips)*
Wonder what it is.

JENNY
(Little laugh)
Well, open it and see.

RICHARD
(Picks it up again, looks it over)
Special delivery, doesn't say where from.

JENNY
Well, open it, for heaven sakes.

RICHARD
(Tries to break twine, can't)
It's . . . ·tied up so . . .
*(Takes a pocket knife, saws through twine, begins to
unwrap. JENNY keeps a distance. RICHARD reveals
contents. Slow awe in movements)*

JENNY
(Trying for unconcern)
What, what *is* it?

RICHARD
(Wonder)
Jenny! Look!

JENNY
Hm?

RICHARD
Jenny! It's money!

JENNY
It's what?

RICHARD
IT'S MONEY!!

JENNY
(Feigning disbelief and childish pleasure)
Money. It's money?

RICHARD
(Subdued; awe)
Jenny; it's money. It's a great deal of money.

JENNY
(Taking a step closer)
Well, for . . . for heaven sake.

RICHARD
Jenny, it's ten-dollar bills, wrapped in packages of five hundred dollars each.

JENNY
(Beautiful bewilderment)
Well . . . how *much?* How much *is* there?

RICHARD
(Starts counting, aloud then silently)
One, two, three, four, five, six, seven, eight, nine . . .

JENNY
(During his counting. Pauses between)
How . . . how incredible. I've . . . How absolutely incredible.

RICHARD
And wait . . . Here are hundred-dollar bills. One, two, three, four . . . *(Slight confusion)* Forty-nine hundred dollars.

JENNY
(Some confusion)
Forty-nine?

RICHARD
Jenny, there's almost five thousand dollars here. Four thousand, nine hundred dollars. Jenny! Four thousand, nine hundred dollars!

JENNY
Well, that's incredible! Not five thousand?

RICHARD
(Sudden suspicion something's wrong)
I don't get it.

JENNY
Aren't you . . . aren't you pleased?

RICHARD
(Wry comment on her word)
Pleased!? I don't know whether I'm pleased or not.

JENNY
(Still not near the money)
Is it real? Is it real money?

RICHARD
(Looks at a bill)
Yes; of course it's real: real used hundred-dollar bills.

JENNY
(A kind of satisfaction)
My God.

RICHARD
But . . . but *why?* I mean, there's no *sense* to it.

JENNY
(A protective step forward)
Yes, but it *is money.*

RICHARD
(Looks at it glumly)
It's money, all right. Too bad we can't keep it.

JENNY
What do you mean?

RICHARD
(No great enthusiasm)
I mean we can't keep it. I'll take it to the police.

JENNY
No!

RICHARD
I *have* to, Jenny. There's something wrong here.

JENNY
What!

RICHARD
(At a loss for words)
Well . . . I mean . . .

JENNY
It's addressed to you, isn't it? It came special delivery; it's
not as though you *found* it, for God's sake.

RICHARD
Yes, I know, but . . .

JENNY
(As offhand as likely)
Well, it seems to me someone wants you to have it. I . . . I
can't think of any other reason for someone to send it to
you.

RICHARD
Wants me to *have* it. Yes, but who?

JENNY
I . . . I don't know. *(Shrugs)* Someone.

RICHARD
Look, it could be something awful like . . .

JENNY

Like what?

RICHARD

Like, like the Mafia, or something, or bank robbers, or . . .
sent it here for safekeeping, and . . .

JENNY
(Laughs gaily)

Don't be ridiculous.

RICHARD
(Thinks about it; subdued)

You think someone *sent* it to me?

JENNY
(The most obvious thing in the world)

Of *course.*

RICHARD

Yes, but *who?*

JENNY

Well . . . maybe . . . somebody you did something for.

RICHARD

Those sort of things don't happen . . . not to *me.*

JENNY

Well, *this* has happened.

RICHARD
(Holds the money out to her; quite childlike)

Don't you want to . . . touch it, or anything?

JENNY

Oh. Yes; of course. *(Goes to him, touches the money, smiles
faintly)* I wonder who sent it to you.

RICHARD
I . . . I don't *know*. There's a man I sit next to on the train a lot. *He* seems very interested in me; older fellow, banker type. Keeps asking me about my work, how I manage. Maybe, maybe he's a millionaire, and maybe he's sort of crazy.

JENNY
(Unlit cigarette out)
Match.

RICHARD
Hm? Oh, yeah. *(Is about to hand her the matchbook, thinks better of it, lights her cigarette)* It could come from somebody like him.

JENNY
(Slightest doubt)
Well, yes, it could.

RICHARD
(Puzzled, a little deflated)
And then again it couldn't. I mean, probably didn't.

JENNY
(Comforting)
Yes. But someone.

RICHARD
Yes. *(Considers, gives her a bill)* Here. For you.

JENNY
(Tiniest pause)
Thank you. You're . . . you're not going to turn it over to the police, then.

RICHARD
(Pause, slight guilt, but bravura)
No, I don't think so. *(Pause)* I guess someone wants me to

have it. Someone *must*. It'd be silly not to keep it. *(Pause)*
Don't you think so?

JENNY
(Nice smile)

Yes. I think so.

RICHARD

I mean, it would be stupid to just . . . throw it away.

JENNY

Yes; it would be. *(Cheerful)* Let's have a drink: to celebrate?

RICHARD
(The sky has cleared)

Yes! Let's.

JENNY
(Moves toward hall)

I'll get the ice.

RICHARD
(Moves toward the liquor cabinet)

Good— And I'll make us a four-thousand-nine-hundred-dol-
lar martini.

JENNY

Super! *(Exiting)* Call it five thousand even; sounds so much
nicer.
     *(JACK enters through the french doors after JENNY
     exits and RICHARD follows)*

JACK
(Sauntering into the room; addresses the audience)

The months turn; people live and die, but I just . . . wander
around. I tell you, there are days when I admit to myself that
I don't think I'm alive—never have been. *Un voyeur de la*

vie . . . that's me. Look on; look in. *(Propounds a great truth, with nothing other than objectivity)* I've never felt really alive. It can't be only the isolation, the isolation of money, do you know? Naw, can't be that. I know lots of people with much more than I've got, and they've been alive . . . killed themselves and everything! Oh, by the way, I did what I said I was going to. *(Nods)* I made my will—remade it, to be technical—and left the whole kaboodle to Jenny and Richard here. Three million plus. I'd better not tell them, though. It's hard enough to like me as it is. I mean, I'm likable and all, but . . . *(Spies the money on the table)* My goodness. *(Speaks loudly, is now in the action)* My goodness! Look at all that money!

RICHARD
(Enters from kitchen)
DON'T TOUCH THAT!

JACK
(Feigned affront)
I'm sorry!

RICHARD
(Still stern, advances toward the money)
Just don't touch it.

JACK
Well. Shall I go back out and knock?

RICHARD
(Sighs, laughs a little)
I'm sorry, Jack.
(JENNY re-enters, with the ice bucket)

JENNY
Here we go, five thousand dollars' worth of ice, an . . . oh. Jack.

JACK
(Sees they are both ill at ease. To audience)
My goodness.

JENNY
(Tiny pause; show of great bonhomie)
Hi!

RICHARD
Join us.

JACK
(Smiles, waiting to have things explained)
O.K.

RICHARD
(To JENNY)
Jack, uh, noticed the money here, and . . .

JACK
(Very pleasantly)
. . . and practically got my head snapped off.

JENNY
Oh. Well; there it is; money.

JACK
(Looks at it)
Did you steal it, or make it in the basement on your own
little press?

RICHARD
Neither, we . . .

JENNY
It arrived; it just . . . arrived.

RICHARD
(To explain further)

In the mail.

JENNY

Yes.

RICHARD
(Ibid.)

Special delivery.

JENNY

Yes.

JACK
(Tiny pause; clearly, there must be more explanation)
Well, that's very nice.

JENNY
Someone sent it to Richard.

JACK

Oh?

RICHARD

Yes.

JACK

Who?

JENNY
Well, we don't know, someone, we figure, who . . . well,
appreciates him. Admires him, maybe.

JACK
You mean you have no idea where it came from.

JENNY

No.

RICHARD

None.

JENNY

Absolutely none.

JACK

Is there a lot? Can I touch it?

RICHARD
(Involuntary gesture to protect money, withdraws it)
Sure.

JACK
(Touches it with one finger, looks at finger)
Perfectly dry.

JENNY

Of course; it's real.

RICHARD
(Sudden, none-too-happy thought)
Jack . . . *you* didn't do this, did you?

JACK

Do what?

RICHARD
You didn't. *You* didn't send us this money, did you?

JACK
(Tiny pause, then a laugh)
Christ, no!

RICHARD

You're sure, because if you did . . .

JACK

I'm sure; I'm absolutely sure. *(To audience)* I didn't, by the way; I didn't send it to them. *(Back to them)* How much is there?

JENNY

Nearly . . .

RICHARD

Five thousand.

JACK

Well, that should prove it to you. I never deal in small amounts.

RICHARD
(Defensive)

It might seem a small amount to *you*, but, to *some* people . . .

JENNY
(To change the subject)

Why don't we all have a nice martini?

JACK

Splendid!
>   (RICHARD *sets about to make them.* JENNY *straightens
>   up the room)*

I didn't mean to ridicule your . . . your windfall.

JENNY

Oh, now . . .

JACK

It's just splendid. *(To the audience)* And damned peculiar
too, if you ask me. *(Back into the action)* Well, I *do* hope
you're going to give a party.

(RICHARD *and* JENNY *look at one another, enthusiasm first)*

JENNY

Why, yes; we could!

RICHARD
(Hesitating)

Well, I don't think we ought to announce that . . .

JACK

No, just a party for the hell of it. Live it up a little! Get some
caviar! Serve champagne! Hire a butler! Give a garden party!

JENNY
(Entranced)

A garden party!

RICHARD
(Giving over to it)

Sure! Why not!

JACK

Sure! Why not! *(To the audience; shrugs)* Why not?

JENNY

What a super idea. When?

JACK

Now.

JENNY

Well, no . . . Next week, and . . .

RICHARD
(Wistful; a little sad)
You know . . . people make plans, and . . .

JACK
No; *now*. This very minute: white heat. Get on the phone.
Give a blow-out; just for the hell of it! *(Gentler)* Do something wild, and out-of-the-ordinary, and . . . the sort of
thing you've always *wished* you could do.

JENNY
Yes! Let's! I'll call . . . who shall I call?

RICHARD
Well . . . Chuck and Beryl . . .

JENNY
(On her fingers; enthusiasm)
Yes, Chuck and Beryl, and Cynthia and Perry, too, of
course . . .

RICHARD
. . . yes . . .

JENNY
. . . and . . . and Gilbert and Louise. Who else?

RICHARD
(Little laugh)
Hey, come on now. Let's not spend it all in one place.

JENNY
Is that enough? Six? Oh, and Jack; *you'll* come, Jack.

JACK
No, my darling; I've got a serious game of backgammon at
the club.

JENNY

. . . oooohhhh . . .

JACK

No; *very* serious. High stakes. Wouldn't miss it for the world.

JENNY
(A colt)

I'll go call. O.K.?

RICHARD
(Amused)

O.K.

JENNY
(To RICHARD*)*

You figure out what we need, how much liquor and all . . .

RICHARD

Not champagne?

JENNY

Yes! Of course! But some people don't like it. I'll go call.
(Starts out of the livingroom)

RICHARD

What time?

JENNY

Oh . . . six, six-thirty. What is it now?

RICHARD

Four.

JENNY
(Momentary pause)
Oh. *(Resolve)* Well, better hurry. *(As she goes)* Bye, Jack!

JACK

Bye! (*To* RICHARD) Does that mean I'm supposed to be gone
by the time she gets back from phoning?

RICHARD
(*Merely laughs; hands* JACK *his martini*)
Here.

JACK
(*Takes it*)
Ice-cold, juniper-berried heaven. Thank you.
(*We will hear* JENNY *faintly from the other room,
talking to people on the phone. We will hear her
enthusiasm*)

RICHARD

She's so excited. Cheers.

JACK

Double. Well, why shouldn't she be? Quite marvelous *getting*
money this way.

RICHARD

Yes.

JACK

No tax, I mean. Tax-free?

RICHARD

Hm?

JACK

Well, you won't de*clare* it, of course . . . and that way
there's no tax.

RICHARD
(*He'd never thought of that*)
You're right! Free and clear. God!

JACK

And maybe there'll be *more*.

RICHARD
(*A little puzzled*)

More? Why?

JACK

Well, good God . . . if someone's sending you money like
this, why should they stop with one bundle? Maybe you'll
get it every week.

RICHARD
(*Almost blushes*)

Oh, come on.

JACK

No; I mean it!

RICHARD
(*Worried frown*)

Jack, you won't . . . you won't tell anybody about this, will
you?

JACK
(*Jaunty*)

My dearest Richard . . . it'll fly out of mind in thirty sec-
onds. No, of *course* I won't say anything. I don't want to
screw it up for you.

RICHARD

I mean not even casually, or reference to it, you know, at the
club, or . . .

JACK

. . . or when I've had a drink or two? No, Richard; I won't.
I promise.

RICHARD

Thanks.

JACK
(*Lolling*)
Money is a curious thing, isn't it, Richard?

RICHARD
(*Small boy*)
I don't know; I've never had too much.

JACK
No: the thing and the symbol. It's a piece of paper, with ink on it . . . and the ink and the paper together aren't worth a quarter of a cent—less . . . yet if we didn't have it, the world would stop.

RICHARD
We could go back to barter.

JACK
Yes, I suppose we could. It's like painting. A stretch of canvas and some paint. Worth what? Four dollars? Five? Yet put a value on it. Let *me* do it, and it sells for a certain sum, or someone else, and ten times more . . . a hundred! A certain Picasso for half a million? Not a bad painting, *worth* it, maybe. Money. How much does a cow sell for?

RICHARD
I don't know . . . two hundred dollars?

JACK
Maybe. Let's say. One Picasso painting for twenty-five hundred cows. All that milk. How many gallons does a cow give off in a day?

RICHARD
Fifteen?

JACK
(Some astonishment)

Gallons?

RICHARD

No. Quarts. I think I read it.

JACK

O.K. *(Figures in his head)* That comes to . . . fifteen times
twenty-five hundred is . . .

RICHARD

You want a pencil and paper?

JACK
(Figures; waves him off)

. . . figuring three hundred and *sixty* days a year, giving the
cows holidays off. Thirty-seven-five times thirty-six and carry
all those zeros . . . comes to . . . good God! Thirteen and
a half million quarts of milk in a year.

RICHARD

You're kidding!

JACK

No; I'm not. Thirteen million and a half quarts of milk in
one year.

RICHARD

That's incredible!

JACK

It is, isn't it. How much does milk go for wholesale?

RICHARD

Ten cents?

JACK

No, less. There's all that awful mark-up before it gets to us.
Let's say five cents. Thirteen-five by twenty . . . this is even
more fascinating! Nearly seven hundred thousand dollars a
year for the milk alone!

RICHARD

What are you getting at?

JACK

Which would you rather have? The Picasso or the cows?

RICHARD
(Thinks, shakes his head; genuine)
I don't know. Another drink?

JACK
(Gulps his down, simultaneously shaking his head)
No. I've got to get to the club. Old Digby's waiting, panting
at the backgammon board.

RICHARD

Oh. O.K.

JACK
(Both have risen; stops)
Now that's the *interesting* thing. Old Digby. Do you know
that he's eighty-seven, by the way? He *adores* money . . .
and not as a symbol . . . as a *thing* in itself. I'll bet he's got
sixty million if he's got one, but it's all a *thing* with *him*. It
doesn't become Picassos or cows or . . . anything but just the
paper as paper. Money as money.

RICHARD
(Pause, almost apologetic)
Money *is* money, you know.

JACK
(Apologetic; gentle)

I *know* it is.

RICHARD
(Quietly dogmatic)

It's paying for this house, and a good education for Roger, and something every once in a while to make Jenny happy . . .

JACK

I *know;* I *know*.

RICHARD
(Indicates the money on the desk)

So, when something like *this* comes along . . . well, it means something.

JACK

I wasn't making fun of you.

RICHARD

Don't tell Jenny, but I might be able to get her some kind of greenhouse, a small one . . .

JACK

I told you: not a word about anything. Money? *What* money? I've got to go. *(Starts out french doors)* It just occurred to me that I don't think I've ever used the front door in this place. Is it nice?

RICHARD

The front door?

JACK

Mmm.

RICHARD
(He'd never really thought about it before)
Well, *yes* . . . it's all right, I guess.

JACK
I must do it someday.

RICHARD
Jack?

(JACK stops, half out)
Nothing.

JACK
(As RICHARD turns away; to the audience)
He's *right*; and I *wasn't* making fun of him. Money . . . is
. . . money. See you. *(Exits)*

JENNY
(Bounces back in)
Are you two . . . ? Oh. Is Jack gone?

RICHARD
Um-hum.

JENNY
(Sort of breathless)
Chuck and Beryl are coming; they were going to just sort of
sit around; and I got Cynthia and Perry, or I got Cynthia,
rather, and they had to get out of something, but they'll be
here, too, and I'm trying Gil and Louise but their line keeps
being busy, so I'll go back and finish *that* up.

RICHARD
O.K. You want a martini now?

JENNY
No; when I come back. *(As she goes again)* Roger should be
arriving soon. He'll have to take a taxi from the station.

RICHARD

A *taxi!?*

JENNY
(Pauses her flight momentarily)
Yes; a taxi. *(Indicates the money)* Don't you think we can
afford one?

RICHARD
(It sinks in; he laughs sheepishly)
Oh. Hunh! Yes, I guess we can.
(JENNY exits)
*(RICHARD looks at the money, straightens it out;
reaches in his pocket for a cigarette, finds none,
looks around for one. Finds a cigarette box empty,
looks some more)*

RICHARD
(Half calling)
Jenny, where did you put the cigarettes? Never mind, I can
find them.
*(Hands on hips for a moment, pondering. Goes to—
what? a side table, maybe, opens a drawer, looks in,
rummages, suddenly halts, frozen. Puts his hand on
something, slowly brings it out. It is a bundle of
money. He looks at it, looks over to the pile on the
table, looks back at the money in his hand, drops
the new bundle down on a chair, or the sofa, which-
ever is handier, and looks around the room, spies
JENNY's sewing basket—say—and goes over to it;
hesitates just a moment, then opens it, reaches in,
takes out yet another bundle of money which he
regards with a curious intensity as he takes it over
and dumps it down where he put the last. Spies a
box on the mantel and goes to it, opens it, and
comes up with a fistful of money. He lets it fall, like
confetti, all around him)*

JENNY
(Re-enters)

Well, that's done. Gilbert and Louise are coming, too, so that makes . . . *(She stops, sees what he has found)* . . . everybody we asked.

RICHARD
(In a kind of a fog)

Jenny; look. What *is* it?

JENNY

Money, Richard.

RICHARD

But . . . is it . . . is it yours?

JENNY

There isn't time to tell you now, I . . .

RICHARD

Yes. There is. You must.

JENNY

We have so much to do before . . .

RICHARD

Wait! *(Points to the money on the table)* Did you send me that package?

JENNY

Actually, yes . . . well, I *had* to; there was *so* much, and I couldn't think of any way to . . .

RICHARD

Have you been . . . have you been *gambling?*

JENNY
(Jumping on that)

Yes!

RICHARD

Where? On what? Who through?

JENNY

There's . . . there's this man.

RICHARD

Called?

JENNY

What does it matter so long as I've been winning?

RICHARD
(Steelier)

Called?

JENNY

Desorio.

RICHARD

That's a lie.

JENNY

Don't you *talk* to me like that!

RICHARD

Isn't it a lie?

JENNY

Well . . . sort of.

RICHARD

THEN IT'S A LIE!

JENNY
(Shrugs)

Yes.

RICHARD

How much is there here? There's thousands!! Where did you get it?

JENNY
(Defensive)

I didn't *steal* it.

RICHARD
(Steely)

Where did you *get* it!?

JENNY

I earned it.

RICHARD

A job! You've got a job!

JENNY

Sort of.

RICHARD

I *told* you I didn't want you to take a *job*. No! You couldn't have earned this at a job. There's too much! There's thousands of dollars here, and . . .

JENNY

Six months!

RICHARD
(Laughs ruefully and half hysterically)

No, look, darling; look. Tell me. Did . . . did someone leave it to you? Did someone die and you haven't told me?

JENNY

Nobody died. I earned it. *(Slight pause)* In the afternoons.

RICHARD

Look; sweetheart: even if you worked full-*time* you couldn't
have earned *this* kind of money. Come on now; *tell* me.

JENNY
(Miffed and playing for time)
Oh? Really? I guess *not* if all I'm supposed to be good for is
a domestic or something.

RICHARD
(Gritting his teeth)
Where did you *get* it?

JENNY
(Sighs, rattles it off)
I make two hundred dollars an afternoon, four days a week,
sometimes more. I've spent a little on clothes, but there
hasn't been time to *spend* the rest, and . . .

RICHARD

Nobody pays that sort of money! I mean you've no training.

JENNY

You don't *need* any.

RICHARD
(Bewildered, and getting angry at the mystery)
What *do* you need?

JENNY

Where's my martini? You promised me an ice-cold, super-
special . . .

RICHARD
(Grabs her arm)
Now tell me!

JENNY

Ow! Now let go of me!
*(He does; she rubs her arm as they glare at each
other. Subdued)*
There's nothing worth telling.

RICHARD

By God, you tell me or I'll make a bonfire of this money in
the middle of the lawn!

JENNY
(Pleading underneath)
Don't be ridiculous! It's money!

RICHARD

I want to know where it comes from!

JENNY
(Her voice rising, too)
It comes from a job!

RICHARD

What *kind* of a job!?

JENNY
(Wild hunting)
A . . . a receptionist.

RICHARD

For *that* kind of money? *(Snorts-sneers)*

JENNY

It's a very expensive place!

RICHARD

What *sort* of expensive place?!

JENNY

A . . . a doctor's office.

RICHARD

You expect me to believe you sit behind the desk at some
god-damn doctor's office a couple of hours in the afternoon,
and you get two hundred dollars a day for it?! You must
think I'm crazy!!

JENNY

It's a very special and very expensive place!

RICHARD
(A *little fearful, a little disgusted*)
What, what is it, some kind of . . . of abortionist office, or
something?

JENNY

My God, you're disgusting!

RICHARD

Why! I've read in the paper of a man found out his wife
worked for an abortionist, brought him patients, as a matter
of fact.

JENNY

You're disgusting!!

RICHARD

Well, I'm *sorry*; but if you're going to be so damned secretive,
what am I *supposed* to think? Hunh?

JENNY
(*Trapped and furious*)
Think what you like!! (*Quite cutting*) Don't you want the
money?

RICHARD
(Both furious now)
The money's got nothing to do with it!

JENNY
Oh yes it has! You don't think I do it for pleasure, do you?

RICHARD
Do what!? Sit behind a desk!?

JENNY
Yes; sit behind a desk!

RICHARD
What's the name of this place?

JENNY
(Daring him)
No name; just a number.

RICHARD
Yeah? Well, what's the number?

JENNY
It's confidential!

RICHARD
I'm your husband!

JENNY
I'm your wife! Do you tell me everything?

RICHARD
I like being told the truth!

JENNY
How much do you talk about *your* job? To *me*.

RICHARD

It's a dull job!

JENNY

So's mine!

RICHARD

The money isn't! The money isn't so damn dull! Christ! It's four times what *I* get. (*Contemptuous*) Sitting behind the desk in a doctor's office . . . sounds more like a high-class whorehouse!

JENNY

I don't *like* that word.

RICHARD

Whorehouse! Call house! Cat house!
    (*There is a silence.* JENNY *looks out toward the garden.* RICHARD *begins to realize he's hit on it*)
No; look; come on; what is it *really*?

JENNY
(*Looking away; sort of wistful, sad*)
Just a place.

RICHARD

A place.

JENNY

Where they pay me.

RICHARD
(*Grabs her arm again*)
For God's sake! What do they pay me for!?

JENNY

It's *me* they *pay*! (*Long pause; sort of lost*) Don't you want the money?

RICHARD
(Lets go of her arm, backs away a little, shakes his head; stuttered, almost laughing disbelief)
I, I don't . . . I don't believe it. I, I don't believe it.

JENNY
(Quite light)
Then don't.

RICHARD
(Backs a bit further away; same confusion)
I, I can't *believe it.* I CAN'T.

JENNY
(Coming toward him; the nicest smile)
Darling, it's going to make such a tremendous difference.

RICHARD
(Laughing mirthlessly at the irony)
Oh, by God it is!

JENNY
(Still happy; occupied)
All the things we've been wanting for years . . .

RICHARD
We!

JENNY
We can have a second car, and . . .

RICHARD
There's no . . . I don't believe this!

JENNY
There's no what?

RICHARD

Room in the garage. *(Incredulous)* How could you *do* such a thing!? *(Pause)* Come on, it *isn't* true, *is* it?

(JENNY nods, slowly)

No; is it? Really?

JENNY

(Dogmatic; impatient)

It is for *us*; for everything we *want!*

RICHARD

(Between set teeth; quiet rage, letting it sink in firmly)

You are my wife; and Roger's mother; and you are a common *prostitute!?*

JENNY

That's a *horrid* way to *put* it.

RICHARD

HOW THE HELL AM I SUPPOSED TO PUT IT!!?

JENNY

I'm not the only *one*, you know. I'm not the only person in the world who . . .

RICHARD

You're the only one who's married to *me!*

JENNY

(Triste reasoning)

But it doesn't make any difference to *us*, and . . .

RICHARD

(Hard)

Doesn't it? *(Walks over to her, slaps her hard across the face)* Doesn't it? How much do you charge for *that?* *(She just stares at him, firm but maybe near tears way underneath. So he slaps her again, just as hard)* I said: how much do you charge for that!!

JENNY
(Says nothing, really, maybe a kind of growl-cry as she slaps him back, just as hard as he hit her)

RICHARD
(Cold, after a moment's pause)
Get out. Pack up and get out of here.

JENNY
(Equally cold)
Where!

RICHARD
Anywhere! Or I will. No, by God, I won't! It's my house, I paid for it. I stay here!

JENNY
(Curiously unemotional)
I can't . . . just like that.

RICHARD
I said get out!

JENNY
A lot of things here are mine.

RICHARD
Take them! Take them!

JENNY
(Through her teeth)
You certainly don't expect me to get everything together right now and . . .

RICHARD

I'll send it after you! Just . . . just get out!

JENNY

No, no, you wouldn't. I know *you:* you can never manage anything like that. I'm the one who has to get the movers and arrange everything, and . . .

RICHARD

CRAP!!

JENNY

Well, it's perfectly true. When your aunt what's-her-name wanted her big, ugly breakfront back, you said you'd take care of it, and *weeks* went by and you didn't do a damn thing.

RICHARD
(Quietly, with controlled rage)
Get your things together and get out of this house!

JENNY
(Tired of it all)
Oh, don't be silly.

RICHARD
(Fury and disbelief)
Don't be *what!?*

JENNY
I said, don't be silly. Give me a cigarette.

RICHARD
You god-damn wanton bitch!

JENNY
I am *not* wanton! I told you: it's for the money! The money *you* don't make! The money we *need!* You think I get any enjoyment out of it?

RICHARD

Think!? I, I, I, I. I don't think anything! I *can't!* I'd go stark raving mad if I thought! Men kill their wives for this sort of thing!

JENNY
(Giggles)

Oh, darling . . .

RICHARD
(Mocked, becomes uncontrollable)

You don't think they do? *(Starts toward her with serious intent)* Read the papers and find out! By God, read tomorrow's papers and find . . .
(They are both stopped by the sound of the front door slamming. ROGER enters, from the hallway)

ROGER

Hi! I took a taxi; do you have any money?

JENNY
(As if she'd forgotten all about him and is sorry)

Roger!

ROGER

The taxi driver says he wants five dollars over the fare because it was such a long way.

RICHARD
(Fury turned on driver)

Oh, he does, does he? *Well*, I'll fix that son of a bitch.
(RICHARD exits, maybe pushing ROGER to one side as he goes)

ROGER
(Looks at RICHARD's exit, confused; back to JENNY; genuine affection)

Hi, Mom.

JENNY
(Embarrassed, but covering)
Darling! You're so . . . so terribly early.

ROGER
(Statement of fact)
The train was on *time*.

JENNY
(A little flustered)
Oh? Was it? Well, then . . . our clock must be slow.

ROGER
Must be. *(Goes to a chair, stands on its seat, looks out through french windows over fence.)* How's the tennis?

JENNY
What tennis?

ROGER
(Points)
At the club.
                    (Angry voices from outside front door)

JENNY
(Looks off apprehensively)
Oh, I . . . I don't pay much attention.

ROGER
Dad been playing? I hope the cab driver doesn't kill him.

JENNY
(Calling off; worried)
Richard? *(To* ROGER*)* Get *down* off that before your father sees you!

ROGER
O.K. . . . *(Jumps down; sees the money)* Wow! Is that money?

JENNY
(Preoccupied, defensive)
Yes, now . . . just leave it be.

ROGER
What is it, the sweepstakes?

JENNY
Just . . . don't concern yourself, now.

ROGER
Can I have a bunch?

JENNY
(Sudden anger)
No! Now let it alone!

ROGER
(Hurt, some)
I'm sorry. *(Heavy-handed irony)* Gee, am *I* glad *I* came home.

JENNY
(Apologetic)
Oh, Roger, darling, I'm . . .
(RICHARD *reappears, a little mussed*)

RICHARD
(Vengefulness and pride)
I hit him!

ROGER
(Shy)
Hi, Dad.

RICHARD
(To JENNY, *since she caused it)*
I hit the son of a bitch!

JENNY
(Quite rebuking)
Did you say hello to your son?

RICHARD
Hm?

ROGER
(Shy, pleased)
Hi.

RICHARD
(Really sees ROGER for the first time; sadness and pride) Hi.
(Back to JENNY; quiet fury and glee) I hit that son of a
bitch.

JENNY
(Quietly desperate)
Why!

RICHARD
Why!!? He wanted nine dollars. The bastard wanted the
regular fare and five dollars extra because . . .

JENNY
That is no reason to hit anyone!

RICHARD
WHO AM I SUPPOSED TO HIT! (Less loud, but no less intense)
Who am I supposed to hit!

ROGER
(To fill a tiny silence)
How's the tennis, Dad?

RICHARD
(To ROGER)
What?

ROGER
(Intimidated)

Tennis. How is it?

RICHARD
(Confused)

I, I haven't . . . I, I, I, haven't played.

ROGER

Un huh . . .

JENNY

You'll get a lawsuit on us, you know.

RICHARD
(Deflated; embarrassed, even)

I only hit him on the shoulder. We . . . we just scuffled
a little.

JENNY
(Pause, disappointment and relief)

Oh.

RICHARD
(A sneer)

Not what I wanted to do.
            (ROGER *has gone up on the chair again*)

ROGER

Wow! Right in the crotch!

RICHARD

Who! What!

JENNY

Roger, don't use words like that.

RICHARD
(Scoffs)

Oh, Jesus!

ROGER

Serve took a bad bounce, hit him right in the . . . what word shall I use?

RICHARD

Don't ask your mother, she's too ladylike. *(Realizes where* ROGER *is)* GET THE HELL OFF THE GOD-DAMNED FURNITURE.
(ROGER does so)

ROGER
(Subdued, unhappy)

Sorry.

RICHARD

You think we're made of money?

ROGER
(Defensive, indicates money all over)

It *looks* like it.
(This sets in an embarrassed silence)

RICHARD
(To change the subject)

Did you have a good term?

ROGER

All right.

RICHARD

What's your average? What did you end up with?

ROGER

C plus.

RICHARD

What did you start out?

ROGER

C plus.

RICHARD
(Bitter)

Keep it up: by the time you're eighteen we won't even be able to get you into an agricultural college!

JENNY

Be nice!
    (RICHARD's *mouth drops open, but he doesn't say any-thing*)
Set the clock right.

RICHARD

It *is* right.

ROGER

It's twenty minutes slow.

RICHARD
(Furious)

Then you set it right!

JENNY

Richard!

RICHARD

Shut up!
    (ROGER *goes to the mantel clock, takes it down*)

ROGER

What do I do?

RICHARD

Turn the knob; turn the god-damn knob!

JENNY

Richard, if you can't be . . .

RICHARD
(Between clenched teeth)

I told you to shut up! *(To* ROGER*)* No! Too far! That's tooo
. . . DON'T TURN IT BACK. *(Disgust, takes the clock, none too
gently, from* ROGER*)* Here; give me the god-damn clock.
NEVER TURN IT BACK! Don't ever turn a clock back!

ROGER
(Flustered, confused)

I'm sorry, I . . .

JENNY

Roger, darling, why don't you take your bag upstairs, and . . .

RICHARD
*(Concentrating, excessively, on the clock; to himself
as well as* ROGER*)*

You *never* turn a clock back; *never*.

JENNY

Why don't you go unpack?

ROGER
(Sullen)

O.K. You've got so much money, I don't see why you don't
go *buy* a clock.

RICHARD

ALL RIGHT!

JENNY

Go unpack and then you can come down and *help* us.

ROGER

You want me to go upstairs, or would you rather I turned around and went right back to school?

RICHARD

GET UPSTAIRS!!

ROGER
(Under his breath)

Christ!

RICHARD

And don't say that!

ROGER
(Standing up to him)

Why not! YOU do! *(Exits)*
(Small silence. RICHARD hurls the clock down on the floor)

JENNY
(Calm, displeased)

That helps.

RICHARD
(Intense, pounding his chest with his fingers)

It helps *me!* ME!!

JENNY
(Closes her eyes for a moment; then all business)

I wish you'd make a list of what we need, what liquor we need.

RICHARD
(Stares at her; quietly)

Whore.

JENNY
(Ignores it)
We'll have champagne, but there are always some people
don't like it, and . . .

RICHARD
(Ibid.)
Whore!

JENNY
. . . and so you'd better check. If we're going to have *fresh*
caviar, and I think we should, then I've got to go down to
Blaustein's and get some . . .

RICHARD
(Ibid.)
Filthy, rotten, no-good little whore!

JENNY
(Quite savage)
Be quiet! You've got Roger in the house!

RICHARD
(Top of his voice)
I'VE GOT A ROTTEN, FILTHY WHORE IN THE HOUSE!

JENNY
(Tiny pause; continues quietly)
Now make a list. They'll be here in about an hour . . .

RICHARD
(Laughing in disbelief)
A party! We're going to have a party!

JENNY
(Level)
Yes; we are.

RICHARD
(The tears that finally come, tears of rage and despair, are incipient; we notice what is coming by a quivering in the voice)

What, what shall we do? Make the announcement? Break it to the neighborhood? Tell them to tell their friends where they can go to get it? Hunh?

JENNY

Make a list.

RICHARD

Hunh? Is that what we should do? Is it? Whore? *(Tears nearer now)*

JENNY

You can phone for the liquor, but we have to know what we need.

RICHARD
(Tears even nearer)

Or, or maybe they already know. Maybe . . . maybe Chuck and Perry and Gil . . . do they . . . do they know already?

JENNY

List.

RICHARD

L, l, list? We . . . all, all right, we need . . . *(Crying commences now)* v, v, v, vodka, and . . .

JENNY
(Gentle)

American or Russian?

RICHARD
(Looks up; pleading)

Both?

JENNY

Both, then.

RICHARD

. . . and . . . and . . . sc, sc, sc, scotch, and . . . bourbon,
and . . . *(Full crying now)* . . . and gin, and . . . gin,
and . . . gin, and . . . *(The word* gin *takes a long time
now, a long, broken word with gasps for breath and the attempt to control the tears)* . . . g—i—i—i—n, and . . .
(Final word, very long, broken, a long howl)
G——i——i——i——i——n——n——n——n.
(Curtain falls slowly as the word continues)

ACT TWO

ACT TWO

(*Set the same; one hour later.* RICHARD *alone on stage, sitting facing out at audience. It might be interesting if he looked the people in the audience right in the eye, but absently, seeing them, but thinking of something else. No attempt to set a new convention (with* RICHARD*), but it will give quite a few people an interesting sensation*)

(JENNY *enters, followed by* ROGER, *both laden with glasses, etc.*)

JENNY
(*Pleasantly incredulous*)
What are you *doing?*

RICHARD
Hm?

JENNY
What are you *doing?* Roger, put those over there and be careful you don't break them.

ROGER
(*Embarrassed at being warned*)
O.K.

JENNY
(*Puts her things down*)
I asked you what you thought you were doing. You've got guests coming over in about ten minutes, and . . .

RICHARD
(*Ugly but quiet; a threat of explosion*)
What am I supposed to do?

ROGER
(Breaks a glass)

Damn!

JENNY

Oh, Roger . . .

RICHARD

That's right! Break the house up!

ROGER

It's only a glass, for God's sake, it . . .

RICHARD

We're not made . . . Do you know how much those things cost?

ROGER
(Standing his ground)

No. How much?

RICHARD
(To JENNY*)*

How much do they cost?

JENNY

Well, they're new, and . . .

RICHARD
(Hint of hysteria; incipience)

They're new!?

JENNY
(Calm)

Yes, and they're crystal, and I suppose they . . . well, I think they were about four-fifty each . . .

RICHARD
(After a pained look at JENNY; *to* ROGER, *shaking his
head and sneering)*
Four-fifty each. You broke a god-damn glass and they cost
four . . .

ROGER
(Digs into his pocket)
Well, here. Take it out of this.

RICHARD
(Unpleasant joy)
Give it to your mother.

JENNY
(Laughing, covering)
Don't be silly, darling. No, Roger, no.

ROGER
(Hand out of pocket again)
Anything to keep peace in the house.

RICHARD
Don't be fresh!

JENNY
(Mollifying; to ROGER)
Darling, go upstairs and change. People *will* be here soon,
and I'll want you to help.

ROGER
Do I have to put on a tie?

RICHARD
(Furious)
Yes!

JENNY
(All on ROGER's *side)*

I'm afraid so, darling. Run along upstairs now.

ROGER

Tie?

RICHARD

Yes; *and* a shirt, *and* trousers, *and* socks, *and* shoes . . .

ROGER
(Going, shaking his head)

Wow.

RICHARD

And don't hang out the window watching the tennis. Change.

ROGER
(Sloppy salute)

Yes, sir! *(Exits)*

RICHARD

And don't salute!

JENNY
(After a tiny pause; reasonable, calm)

It was only a glass.

RICHARD
(Turns on her; quiet wrath)

What have you been doing: buying things behind my back? Crystal? Gold goblets? Clothes?

JENNY

Just a little.

RICHARD

Just a little what!

JENNY
(Sighs)

A few clothes; those glasses; nicer sheets. Didn't you notice?

RICHARD
(Still furious)

Notice what!

JENNY
(Quietly happy)

The nice sheets. I thought they'd . . .

RICHARD

No! I didn't notice the nicer sheets, and by God I won't sleep on them! I won't sleep in the same room with you!

JENNY
(Cool)

And where are you going to sleep?

RICHARD

What?

JENNY

I said, where are you going to sleep? Roger's home, there's no mattress in the guestroom . . .

RICHARD

Why not! Where is it!

JENNY

You threw it out. When you had the hepatitis and you slept in there you said it was awful—the mattress—so we threw it out.

RICHARD

Well, why didn't we get another one!

JENNY
(Shrugs, starts arranging things)
Oh . . . money, or something.

RICHARD

WELL, WE CAN DAMN WELL AFFORD ONE NOW!

JENNY
(Quiet, precise)
I don't see the need. You've told me to get out.

RICHARD
(This stops him for the briefest instant only)
WELL, WHEN ARE YOU GOING!?

JENNY
(Stops what she is doing)
Right now. Right this very minute.

RICHARD

You've got a party! You've got people coming over!

JENNY
(Pretending this complicates things)
Oh. Yes. Well then, I'll leave right after the party, right after everybody goes.

RICHARD

Fine.

JENNY
(Quietly withering)
Or shall I stay and clean up first?

RICHARD

(Can think of nothing for a moment, finally)

Tramp.

JENNY

There's no need for that now.

RICHARD

I can't hold my head up in front of those people; I won't be able to look any of them in the eye. I might scream, or cry, or something.

JENNY

You'll hold your head up. In fact, I should think you might be *able* to look Chuck and Perry and Gil straight in the eye, maybe for the first time.

RICHARD

Why! Because my wife is a whore?

JENNY

(Sort of cajoling)

No . . . well, because for once you won't be the poor relative, so to speak; you can talk about the new car you're going to get, and why don't we raise the dues at the club to keep the riffraff out, and Jenny and I were thinking about Antigua this winter—all those things.

RICHARD

(Some disgust)

You're hopelessly immoral.

JENNY

Not at all! I'm talking about money—that thing that keeps us at each other's throats; that standard of judgment; that measure of a man's worth!

RICHARD

There are other standards!

JENNY

Well, not in the circles *we* move in! Not in *our* environment.

RICHARD

There are *kinds* of money!

JENNY

Yes! Three! Too little, too much, and just enough!

RICHARD

Corrupt!

JENNY

Too much money corrupts; too little corrupts. Just enough? Never.

RICHARD

It's how! *How!*

JENNY

Oh, don't tell me about how! Perry and that real estate he sells? Ten thousand for an acre out near, uh, near the track, and he doesn't even tell the god-damn fools there isn't any city water? Gilbert and his fancy publishing house? What's his advertising budget on trash? Thousands! How much does he spend on a halfway decent book . . . nothing!

RICHARD

All right, all right . . .

JENNY

And you in your research laboratory. All those government contracts? A little work on germ gas maybe?

RICHARD

I told you that in . . . I told you not to say a word about anything I told you . . .

JENNY

You told me in confidence? Well, I'm telling you *back* in confidence! You all stink, you're all killers and whores.

RICHARD
(Nods several times rapidly)
That's quite a performance.

JENNY

You're damned right.

RICHARD
(Great sarcasm)

Bra-*vo!*

JENNY

At least! Come on! More!

RICHARD

With your theories on money, you should have married Jack.

JENNY
(Self-mocking rue)
Unh-hunh; you may be right.

RICHARD

Though I don't necessarily think he'd take any better to having a whore for a wife than I do.

JENNY
(Comforting)
Well, if I'd married Jack none of it would have happened.

RICHARD
(As ROGER *re-enters; starts to go for her)*
Why, you . . .

ROGER
I'm dressed.
(They both pause, for ROGER's *tone has a curious im-
personal disapproval to it)*

JENNY
(Recovering)
And in good time, too. They'll start coming any second. My,
don't you look nice and grown-up.

ROGER
You've seen me in a tie before. *(To* RICHARD*)* Were you
going to hit her?

RICHARD
Mind your own business.

ROGER
(Mildly puzzled)
I thought it was.

RICHARD
Well, it's not. I don't suppose you washed.

ROGER
Well, I didn't have time for a sit-down bath, if that's what
you mean. Why *isn't* it my business?

RICHARD
Because it isn't! Are your fingernails clean?

ROGER
(To JENNY, *the same mildly disapproving curiosity)*
Was he going to hit you? *(Looks at his nails)* Relatively.

JENNY

Don't be silly, darling; your father doesn't hit people bigger
than he is. Come help me with things, now. Those glasses
over there . . .

ROGER
(*Grumbling, sort of*)

People always hit each other when other people are out of
the room.

JENNY
(*Decidedly offended*)

Roger!

RICHARD
(*Snarl*)

Little monster.

ROGER

I wasn't complaining; I was just stating a fact.

RICHARD

Keep your facts to yourself.

JENNY

Nobody hits anybody around here.

RICHARD

Anyway, not above the belt.

JENNY
(*"Not in front of Roger."*)

Richard!

RICHARD
(*Subsiding*)

Sorry! Very sorry. Sorry about everything. Every single thing.

ROGER
(*An aside, to* JENNY)
What's the matter with Dad?

JENNY
(RICHARD *can hear them both, of course*)
Oh, nothing; parties upset your father, that's all.

ROGER
(*Goes to* RICHARD: *genuine*)
I'll help.

RICHARD
(*Looks at him for a moment, then, with a head-shaking laugh that could be confused with mockery, but isn't*)
Oh, boy! Thanks!

ROGER
(*Withdraws a little; stung*)
I'm sorry.

RICHARD
(*Quite furious*)
Roger! I mean it! Thank you!

ROGER
(*A little bewildered*)
O.K.

(*Doorbell rings*)

JENNY
(*Sighs, girds herself*)
Well. Here we go.

RICHARD
(*Little boy*)
I'm going to hate this.

ROGER

Hey, what shall I drink?

RICHARD

Ginger ale.

ROGER

Awww.

JENNY
(Exiting)

I'll go.

RICHARD

Roger, do me a favor.

ROGER

Sure. What?

RICHARD

Grow up right.
    (Sounds of greeting from hallway)

ROGER
(Offhand)

O.K. Got any ideas?

RICHARD

Just . . . be good.

ROGER

As the twig is bent, as they say.
    (JENNY re-enters with CHUCK and BERYL)

BERYL
(To JENNY, as they enter)

No, it's been lovely, but I would love some rain. Our lawn
is all brown and splotchy.

JENNY

Oh? Well, we manage ours.

BERYL

Green thumb, my darling.

CHUCK

Won't be any rain till we take off for . . . *Hello*, Richard!

RICHARD
(Shy)

Hi, Chuck; Beryl?

BERYL

Are we too early? I told Chuck we'd be first here.

JENNY

Don't be silly.

CHUCK

And I said, so what? First to come, last to leave; no breeding.
Roger!

ROGER

Hello.

BERYL
(To ROGER; *some wonder)*

Do you grow each time I see you?

ROGER

Probably; I don't see you very much.

JENNY

He grows fresher each time you see him, I can tell you *that*.

CHUCK
(Formality)

How's school, Roger?

ROGER

Fine.

CHUCK

Back for vacation? Now, that's a silly question. Got any silly
answers?

ROGER

I keep those for exams.

(Some laughter)

RICHARD

How true. Hey! How about a drink? Champagne or proper
stuff?

CHUCK
(Hearty)

Champagne!

BERYL
(To CHUCK*)*

You know what it does. *(To* JENNY*)* Keeps him up all night;
bent double. Gas?

CHUCK
(To RICHARD*; ruefully)*

I guess I better have some scotch.

RICHARD

Right. Beryl? *(Goes to her)*

ROGER

Can I help?

BERYL
(Examining caviar; to JENNY*)*

Fresh, how nice. Do you get yours in the city?

JENNY

No, Blaustein's has the fresh.

BERYL
(*To* RICHARD)

Gin, darling, and a little ice. (*Back to* JENNY) Well, fresh
caviar can't keep, and I don't trust Blaustein's.

JENNY
(*A tiny bit of pique*)

Oh, it's perfectly fresh.

BERYL
(*Slight laugh*)

I'm sure it is. I just think Blaustein's cheats a little . . .
keeps it on ice a day or two more than they . . .

JENNY

Would you like some caviar, Chuck?

CHUCK

Sure would. (*Goes to it*) Toast?
Toast?

JENNY

No; crackers.

BERYL
(*Moving away from caviar, looks at garden, expansive*)

How do you keep it!? How do you battle the weeds, and
prune and dust . . . ?

JENNY
(*Proud*)

Green *thumb*.

CHUCK

Cheers!

THE OTHERS
(Nearly simultaneously)

Cheers!

BERYL

While I've got you now, I need you for the blood bank.

JENNY

Richard can't.

BERYL

Why?

JENNY

Hepatitis. And Roger shouldn't, either; he needs all he's got.

ROGER

I don't mind giving blood.

JENNY
(Light, but firm)

I don't think you *should*, Roger.

BERYL

Well, Jenny, then you'll have to give for the whole family.

RICHARD

I don't think she should.

BERYL

Why ever not?

JENNY

Yes. Why not?

RICHARD
(Dogmatic)
I just don't think you should.

JENNY
(A little annoyed)
Well, do you have a reason? Or are you just hoarding everybody's blood.

RICHARD
(Too much attempt at a joke; only JENNY *will see what he means)*
Well, no; you . . . you might have some awful disease for all *you* know.

BERYL
(As CHUCK *laughs)*
Oh, Richard! Really!
(Doorbell)

ROGER
Shall I go?

JENNY
(Exiting; a quick look at RICHARD)
I'll go. Help yourselves to the . . . (*Leaves it unfinished; exits*)

RICHARD
(The tiniest mockery)
How's high finance, Chuck? How's the old market?

CHUCK
Oh, just like marriage . . . up and down, up and down.
*(*BERYL *and* RICHARD *laugh flimsily)*

ROGER
What does *that* mean?

RICHARD

Nothing.

ROGER

Then why did he say it?

RICHARD
(*Annoyed*)
You know perfectly well what it means, so why did you ask?

ROGER
(*Shrugs*)
I thought it was polite. You told me to help.
(JENNY *re-enters, with* GILBERT *and* LOUISE)

JENNY

Richard! It's Gilbert and Louise!

RICHARD

Well! Come on in! You know Beryl and Ch . . .

LOUISE

Yes, I think we've met at the club.

GILBERT

Yes, of course we have.

BERYL

How nice to see you both again.

CHUCK

Drinks are over here. There's champagne *and* the real stuff.

LOUISE

How nice you were to ask us. Oh, will you look at your garden! And the lawn! *How* do you do it?

BERYL

I was commenting before. I *don't* know how they do it.

GILBERT

Who's your gardener? Shropie?

RICHARD

Who?

GILBERT

Shropshire; he has a whole team, and . . .

JENNY

No, we've been doing it ourselves.

LOUISE

We have Shropshire, and they send two men, but we have six acres, too, so that makes a difference.

GILBERT

Charge an arm and a leg.

BERYL

But are they *good*. Chuck and I were thinking of using them, and . . .

CHUCK

Not going to get me mowing weekends . . .

JENNY

It sort of spoils the fun to farm it out—the work . . .

RICHARD
(A *little tentative*)
We, we could have someone in, though.

JENNY
(Secret smile)
Oh? Well, why don't we?

RICHARD
(Bitter at being caught)
Spoils the fun.

JENNY
(To the others)
We thought we might put a greenhouse in, though.

RICHARD
Did we!

LOUISE
Oh, you must. We're so glad *we* did.

JENNY
I've always wanted one.

CHUCK
You must be in the chips, Richard old boy: greenhouse, champagne, caviar . . .

RICHARD
(Laughs lightly)
No; just . . . *(Shrugs, leaves it unfinished)*

JENNY
No, just not scrimping.

BERYL
(Her eyes narrowing slightly)
Oh, I'm glad.

ROGER
(*Weary of asking*)

Can I help?

LOUISE

Roger, *dear!* I didn't even say hello to you. Gilbert! Roger's
here.

GILBERT

Roger, my boy. Home from school?

ROGER
(*False heartiness*)

Yes, Sir!

GILBERT

Doing O.K.?

ROGER

Holding my own, as they say.

GILBERT

Good boy; good boy. Hey, Rich; this is good caviar. Where'd
you get it?

RICHARD

Jenny got it; it's Jenny's.

JENNY

I got it at Blaustein's, just as fresh as if you'd gone into
town and . . .

GILBERT

Damn smart little kike, that Blaustein, putting in caviar
and . . .

ROGER

We don't use words like that around here.
(*Everybody looks at him, not quite sure of what he
means*)
At least, not in the family.

(*Doorbell again*)

JENNY
(*Glad of the chance*)

I'll get it! (*Exits*)

BERYL   LOUISE
(*Both just to say something*)

I still say if you get it in town   The first year we had *our*
it's bound to be fresher.   greenhouse, I was amazed.

RICHARD

Drinks now! Come on, kids; the bar's open.

GILBERT
(*To* RICHARD *as they approach the bar*)

What did I say?

RICHARD   CHUCK
Nothing, nothing.   Your kid's sort of a wiseacre,
                                     hunh?

GILBERT
(*Hurt*)

What did I say?

(*Simultaneous*)

RICHARD   BERYL
Nothing; forget it.   But aren't they a terrible
                                     chore?

CHUCK	LOUISE
I don't get the champagne. What for? What gives?	Well, no; not if you remember things, like water, and air, and heat, and . . .

(Simultaneous)

RICHARD	BERYL
What gives? Nothing.	*(Laughs)* Ah, just a few things like that!

CHUCK	LOUISE
Looks pretty festive to me.	It takes getting used to, that's all.

ROGER
(If anyone cares)

I apologize.

(JENNY *re-enters, with* CYNTHIA *and* PERRY)

JENNY

The stragglers. Cynthia and Perry Straggler.

PERRY

Hi, folks.

ROGER
(To himself)

Folk.

GILBERT

Well, if it isn't old Perry! Hi, Cyn!

CYNTHIA
(Generally)

Hello there!

RICHARD

Bar's here, kids.

CYNTHIA

Well, will you look at all that!

CHUCK

Is it true what I heard, Perr?

PERRY

Probably. What?

CHUCK

You been selling lots to the black folk twice the going price?
(Some laughter, for this is a joke)

PERRY

Not a word of it! Three times the going price, and at that
I don't let 'em have clear title.
(More laughter)

ROGER

There are two Negro boys at school, on scholarship.

GILBERT
(None too pleasant)
Oh yeah? *(To* RICHARD*)* You ought to send your boy to
Choate, Dick. That's a *good* school.

ROGER

There are Negro boys there, too.

GILBERT

You're kidding.

ROGER

Why not? I mean, why am I kidding?

BERYL
(Not snobbish)
It *is* getting to be a problem.

CYNTHIA
I *know.*

LOUISE
(Very serious)
Well . . . it's a time of change.

JENNY
It's time for a drink, that's what it's time for! Cynthia?
Louise?

ROGER
Actually, there won't be any solution to the color problem—
whatever *that* is—until we're all coffee-colored.

BERYL
Roger!

JENNY
Darling!

GILBERT
Where'd you pick up *that* theory?

ROGER
A book.

PERRY
A little knowledge is a dangerous thing, Roger.

CHUCK
Theories that come out of books ought to stay in books.

RICHARD
(*To* ROGER)

Why don't you pass the caviar? I thought you wanted to help.

ROGER

I've been *ask*ing! I've been standing around on my two hind feet asking if I could be any help and everybody's been ignoring me!

RICHARD
(*Put out*)

You've been standing around on your two hind feet in*sult*-ing everybody, that's what you've been standing around do-ing.

ROGER
(*Something of a pout*)

That was after.

CYNTHIA

Oh, let him alone, for heaven sake! He's a sweet boy. How old are you, Roger, dear?

ROGER

I'm twelve.

JENNY

You're fourteen!

RICHARD

He *is* not; he's fifteen.

JENNY

I ought to know how old my own son **is.**

RICHARD

You ought; yes.

CHUCK

Where you going to put the greenhouse, Dick?

RICHARD

Hm? Oh . . . out there. *(Gestures vaguely)*

JENNY
(Rather pointed)

Show them *where*, darling.

RICHARD
(Trapped)

Hm?

LOUISE

Oh, I'd love to see! Show us!

CYNTHIA

Yes! And I want to look at Jenny's roses.
(CYNTHIA *and* LOUISE *start out through french doors;*
PERRY *automatically follows)*

CHUCK

Well, into the garden we go. Somebody bring a bottle of champagne.

GILBERT
(Following CHUCK*)*

Nobody's *drinking* champagne.

CHUCK

Well . . . bring a bottle of scotch.
(The two men laugh, follow the others out)

JENNY
(To RICHARD*)*

Well . . . ?

RICHARD
(Getting it straight)
Show them where we're going to put the greenhouse.

JENNY
(Dazzling if mirthless smile)
Yes.
(Doorbell rings: JENNY *starts)*
Who's that? We didn't ask anyone else.

RICHARD
(Exiting to garden)
It's your party; you figure it out.

JENNY
(To BERYL*)*
I can't imagine who it is. Roger, darling . . . go see.
*(*ROGER *exits through archway)*
Unless it's Jack Foster. He always drops in, and . . .

BERYL
(Starts exiting to garden)
Well, if it is, I'll leave the two of you alone.

JENNY
(Annoyance showing through)
And what is that meant to mean!

BERYL
(Throaty laugh, as she exits)
Nothing, darling; nothing at all.
(We will probably see one or more of the people out in the garden while they admire it and while RICHARD *improvises where the greenhouse will be, but their backs will be to us, and they will not see inside until they return.)*

ROGER
(Re-entering)

It's a woman to see you.

(MRS. TOOTHE *enters;* JENNY *stares at her, open-mouthed)*

MRS. TOOTHE

Good evening, my dear.

(JENNY *just stares)*

I said, good evening, my dear.

JENNY
(Still staring at her)

Roger, go in the garden.

ROGER
(Bland)

Why?

JENNY
(Turns, snaps)

I said go in the garden!

ROGER
(Some disgust, turns on his heel, goes)

Good God!

JENNY
(Appalled)

What do you want?

MRS. TOOTHE

I want to talk. *(Sits)* Ah! That feels good. I do so hate to walk.

JENNY

You can't *come* here; you *must*n't.

MRS. TOOTHE

I know, my dear, it's very indiscreet, but most important.

JENNY
(Anger, and panic underneath)
I'm having a party! Guests!

MRS. TOOTHE

Yes, I see; fine, I'm one of them.

JENNY

No! I'm sorry; no!

MRS. TOOTHE

Why not?

JENNY

They're friends; Richard thinks you're on the hospital committee, and . . .

MRS. TOOTHE

Fine, I'm on the hospital committee.

JENNY

But these are local people, and Beryl is on the hospital committee, and . . .

MRS. TOOTHE

Beryl?

JENNY

Yes, and Louise is too . . . and, and . . .

MRS. TOOTHE

Well, you'll just have to make up something: I'm not from *here*, I'm from . . .

JENNY

Please! Leave!

MRS. TOOTHE
(Firm, coldly polite)
I told you, my dear, it's a matter of considerable importance.
Does your husband know?

JENNY
Yes, I told him today. Oh, my God, if he sees you and knows
who you are, I don't know what he'll . . .

MRS. TOOTHE
Well, he will have to make the best of it. *(Pause, smile)* Will
he not?

JENNY
(The final supplication of her life)
Please! *Please* leave!
                    (BERYL *and* CHUCK *have started back in*)

MRS. TOOTHE
Your guests are coming back.
                    (JENNY *wheels*)

BERYL
(Not noticing MRS. TOOTHE *yet)*
Jenny, my dear, Chuck and I agree: your husband is an angel;
the greenhouse will be absolutely perfect; you'll . . .

JENNY
(Cutting in)
Beryl, Chuck, this is Mrs. Toothe; Richard and I met her
down in St. Thomas last year, and she's come by to say . . .

MRS. TOOTHE
(Quiet smile)
Hello, Beryl, my dear; I have a bone to pick with you.

CHUCK
(As JENNY *watches, openmouthed)*
My God, what's she doing here?

BERYL
(Cool, calm)
Oh? You have?

MRS. TOOTHE
Yes; indeed I have.

JENNY
(Finally, to BERYL, *flabbergasted)*
You!?

BERYL
(As MRS. TOOTHE *chuckles some, quite calm, with a
tiny smile)*
Yes; and you, too, it would seem.

JENNY
(Awe)
My God.
(The others are coming in now, LOUISE, CYNTHIA,
PERRY, GILBERT *and* RICHARD; ROGER *is still outdoors)*

LOUISE
. . . and it seems to me that if you want the afternoon sun,
well, then you'll have to make allowance for it, and . . .
(Sees MRS. TOOTHE)

RICHARD
(All have seen MRS. TOOTHE *save* RICHARD; *all are
staring at her save him)*
It *could* be swung about, I suppose, though we'd have to dig
up someth—*(He sees her, sees the silence; to* MRS. TOOTHE)
Hello; I've seen you before, haven't I?

MRS. TOOTHE
(Very nice)
Yes, but we didn't really meet; I'm Mrs. Toothe. Hello,
Cynthia; Louise, my dear.
(They nod)

RICHARD
(Not getting it yet)
Well, then, you all know each other, and . . .

MRS. TOOTHE
Where were you on Thursday, Beryl dear?

BERYL
I had, I had a headache, and . . .

MRS. TOOTHE
Well, that will cost you a hundred dollars. Someone was
disappointed.

RICHARD
(Not quite dawn yet)
You, you all know each other?

MRS. TOOTHE
Well, yes, I know all these ladies, and I've met their husbands, but I've known them, well, how shall I say . . . I
don't think we've all known before that we all know each
other.

JENNY
(Lame and unhappy)
This is . . . Mrs. Toothe, darling.

GILBERT
(Rather pleased)
Perry, you never told me.

LOUISE

Cynthia, dear, I'm surprised we haven't run into each other in town.

RICHARD
(Piecing it together)

Look, now, does this mean . . .

PERRY
(He, too, rather pleased)

Well, my God.

MRS. TOOTHE
(To RICHARD*)*

And isn't it charming that all my suburban ladies should be under one roof.

RICHARD

All your ladies, and . . . *(To the women) All of you? (To the men)* And *you've* known about it?

GILBERT
(Not quite pleasant)

Well, of course.

PERRY
(Slightly condescending)

Yes; naturally.

BERYL

But how absolutely marvelous none of us has known about the other.

CYNTHIA
(To LOUISE: *mock chiding)*

You and your shopping trips.

LOUISE
(Giggles a little; to BERYL*)*
And all that museum-going.

MRS. TOOTHE
(Businesslike)
Well. Here we all are.

RICHARD
*(Backing off a little; quietly, as if facing a wall of
strange shapes)*
I don't believe it, I . . . I don't believe it, I . . .

JENNY
(Quietly pleading)
. . . Richard . . .

CHUCK
(Shakes his head, chuckles)
Oh, boy! Oh, Jesus Christ! *(Full laughter)*

RICHARD
(To PERRY*)*
You've . . . you've known? All the time?

GILBERT
(Slightly patronizing)
What did you do, just find out?

RICHARD
(Tiny pause, a real scream)
YES!!!!
(Pause)

CHUCK
(Calm, fairly stern)
Get yourself a drink, boy. Quiet down.
*(*CHUCK *pats* RICHARD *on the shoulder, makes for the
bar)*

RICHARD
(Softer; great loss in it now)

Yes!

GILBERT
(Matter-of-fact)
Well, now you know; and now we all know.
(ROGER enters)

ROGER
Hi! You know, Venus is up already? The sun isn't even down yet, and . . .

JENNY
Roger; go get something.

ROGER
M-m'am?

JENNY
Richard? *Do* something?

PERRY
(Digs into his pocket)
Roger, be a good fellow and run over to the club and get me some pipe tobacco, will you?

ROGER
(Senses the silence)
Well . . . sure.

PERRY
And get yourself a Coke, or something.

JENNY
That's a good boy.

ROGER
(Puzzled, slightly reluctant)
O.K. . . . what, what kind?

PERRY

What?

ROGER

What kind of *pipe* tobacco?

PERRY

Ben at the desk; Ben knows; tell him it's for me.

ROGER
(Suspicion, confusion over, bounds out)
O.K. Be back!

RICHARD

Please, all of you, get out.

MRS. TOOTHE

As I said, I'm sorry I've had to come, but there's been trouble.

BERYL

What kind of trouble?

MRS. TOOTHE

So that I daren't use the phone; daren't call you.

PERRY

Police?

MRS. TOOTHE

Yes.

JENNY
(Quiet panic)

Oh, my God.

MRS. TOOTHE

A man named Lurie; detective, I think.

CHUCK

Can't you buy him off?

MRS. TOOTHE

Won't be had.

GILBERT

That's damned odd.

MRS. TOOTHE

Yes; well; nonetheless, he won't.
    (RICHARD *watches all of this from a distance; maybe sits*)

PERRY

Asking questions?

MRS. TOOTHE

No . . . telling me to clear out.

LOUISE

He didn't ask for *names*.

MRS. TOOTHE

It wasn't a *raid*. Besides, he wouldn't get them.

BERYL
    (*Sighs with relief*)

Well.

GILBERT

Yes; there is *that*.

MRS. TOOTHE
(*Brightly*)
I don't believe I've been asked what I would like to drink.
(*Pause*) Have I?

JENNY
(*Quite preoccupied, mostly with what* RICHARD *is
thinking*)
Oh, no; I don't guess you have.

MRS. TOOTHE
(*To* RICHARD)
Unless you have an objection to my . . . wetting my lips
in your house.

RICHARD
(*Almost a monotone; a stunned quality*)
No, you go right ahead; have what you like; there's cham-
pagne, and . . .

MRS. TOOTHE
(*A little laugh*)
Oh, heavens, no, I don't think so. (*To* CHUCK, *who is still near
the bar*) Is there whiskey?

CHUCK
Sure. Neat?

MRS. TOOTHE
Very, and one cube.

CHUCK
No sooner said. (*To* RICHARD; *an afterthought*) O.K. if I . . .
do the honors?

RICHARD
(*As above*)
No, you go right ahead.

CYNTHIA

I think I'd like one, too. Perry?

PERRY

Right.

(Some general movement to refill, hand drinks, etc.)

GILBERT

(To MRS. TOOTHE; *asking more than just his question)*

I . . . I suppose you'll have to . . . move out.

MRS. TOOTHE

I'm gone! I've left already. There'll be a psychiatrist moving in.

BERYL

(Giggles)

That'll be a surprise for the regulars.

CYNTHIA

(Laughing, too)

Oh, Beryl! Really!

PERRY

(Stretching, breathing out)

Well, I guess you'd better hold off on that greenhouse, Dick.

CYNTHIA

Yes, and put away the caviar.

LOUISE

What a shame. *(Afterthought)* What a shame for all of us!

RICHARD

(Barely registering)

Hm?

GILBERT
(Fairly sententious)
Yes . . . things are going to be a little harder for *all* of us.

MRS. TOOTHE
(Sipping her drink)
Why? *(Good spirits)* This sort of thing happens. It's never the end.

BERYL
It's rather different for you: you're used to it.

MRS. TOOTHE
(Speculative)
Ohhhh, one can get used to anything . . . I should say. *(To* RICHARD*)* Wouldn't you say?

RICHARD
Oh, God.

LOUISE
Yes, but one can't get used to the idea of jail, not to mention the newspapers and . . .

CHUCK
Cops are on to you.

PERRY
Where will you go?

MRS. TOOTHE
(Tiniest pause)
Why not . . . out here?

SEVERAL
(Tones of shock, disbelief)
Out here!

MRS. TOOTHE
Why not?

LOUISE
(Quite grand)
Surely you're not serious.

MRS. TOOTHE
Very good train service; respectable . . . countryside . . .

CHUCK
(Not sure)
Yes, there's very good train service, but . . .

MRS. TOOTHE
If one could find some suitable property. *(Looks at* PERRY*)* Do
you think?

PERRY
No, no, this wouldn't do at all . . .

GILBERT
Absolutely not.

MRS. TOOTHE
(Makes as if to get up and go; very businesslike)
Well, then; I shall just have to find a more congenial city;
somewhere where the police are fast asleep or . . . amenable.
I shall miss you ladies, though.

BERYL
(Tentative)
Of course . . . *(Stops)*
PERRY, CYNTHIA, GILBERT
(More or less simultaneously)
Yes?

BERYL
(A little embarrassed, and pleased by the attention)
Well, I was going to say . . . it . . . it couldn't be right
here: I mean right *here:* it could be . . . nearby.

JENNY
(She hasn't spoken for quite a while)
Well, *yes*; it would be . . . *(Leaves it unfinished)*

RICHARD
(As if hearing through fog)
What did you say, Jenny?

BERYL
*(Naked and embarrassed, but if you're in a nudist
colony . . .)*
I was going to say . . .

RICHARD
Yes. Go on.

JENNY
(If JENNY *can physically blush, yet be resolute, fine)*
I was going to say that if it could be out here then . . .
then it would be handy.

RICHARD
What was that last word?

JENNY
(Tiniest pause)
Handy . . . it would he handy.

RICHARD
(Nods, chuckles)
Um-hum. Oh, yes. *(Chuckles some more)* Oh, God, yes.
(A few defeated tears in the words) Especially with Roger

home: you could make it back and do the jelly sandwiches
—now that he's not going to camp, 'cause we want him here,
not 'cause we can't afford it.

MRS. TOOTHE

I think we'd best keep this to a business discussion. Don't
you think?

PERRY

Yes; I think.

CHUCK

Good idea.

MRS. TOOTHE

Something to be talked about amongst us men. Jenny, why
don't you go out and show the girls your roses?

JENNY
(*Occupied with observing* RICHARD)

Hm?

MRS. TOOTHE

Show the girls your roses.

BERYL
(*Leading the way*)

Yes, why don't we see the garden again? There's so much
there; so very much to see.

CYNTHIA

Yes; coming, Louise?

LOUISE
(*Gravely approving the proposition*)

Of course.

MRS. TOOTHE

Jenny?

JENNY
(Loath to leave RICHARD, *but going)*
Well, all right . . . I . . . all right. *(Exits)*
(The men are left now, with MRS. TOOTHE)

RICHARD
(From where he sits; little emotion)
You're a little high-handed, aren't you?

MRS. TOOTHE
(Cheerfully soothing)
It's so much easier without them.

RICHARD

This *is* my house.

GILBERT

Oh, come off it, Richard.

CHUCK

We're lucky we're not all in jail.

MRS. TOOTHE

No, it won't come to that. Who will give me another drink?

PERRY
(Takes her glass)
Whiskey and ice?

MRS. TOOTHE

Yes. *Thank* you. *One* cube.

GILBERT
(To CHUCK)
How much do you stand to lose?

CHUCK
(Rueful laugh)
Too *much*; damn *far* too much.

GILBERT
(Mulling)
Yeeesss. Tax-free? Be able to retire early if you wanted to? If
it kept up? Louise and I talked it over.

RICHARD
(Coming in, now; a neophyte)
You did? You talked it over? Just . . . talked it over?

GILBERT
Of course. Oh, I know how you *feel*; I felt that way . . . for
a little.

CHUCK
Wanted to break the *place* up.

PERRY
(Returning with MRS. TOOTHE's *drink)*
I *did* break the place up. Gave us an excuse to redecorate.

CHUCK
(Settling)
Funny how quickly you get used to the idea.

PERRY
Yes.

CHUCK
And, there *is* the money.

GILBERT
It's going to be a little tough to manage without it . . . *now.*

PERRY

I can't take Martin away from his school at *this* stage . . .

GILBERT

Same with Jeremy; and there's Jennifer's pony. I'm paying
through the nose to keep it at that damn stable, but I can't
sell it . . . she'd *kill* me.

CHUCK
(Fairly grim)

Anybody want to buy a nearly paid-for Aston-Martin?

PERRY

That's the trouble: we're all involved in things. We can't
. . . just stop.

GILBERT

And just between us, I don't mind admitting Louise and I
get along together much better these days.

PERRY

So do Cyn and I. Most of our arguments were over money.

CHUCK

Yes.

MRS. TOOTHE
(To RICHARD*)*

Do you begin to understand better now?

RICHARD
(Still rather numb)

Oh yes; I understand.

MRS. TOOTHE
(Hears the women talking in the garden)

Listen to them. The girls chattering away.

PERRY
(Smiles)

Yes.

MRS. TOOTHE

Shall we talk business?

GILBERT

Right! Richard? Will you be chairman?

RICHARD
(A haze)

Will I what?

GILBERT

Be chairman. We want a proper business meeting.

CHUCK
(Moving in)

Here you are. Besides, it's your chair.

GILBERT

Who will propose him?

CHUCK

I.

PERRY

Seconded.

GILBERT

Carried.

CHUCK

Call the meeting to order, Richard.

RICHARD
(Brief hesitation, then)

Meeting come to order. (*Pause*) Well?

PERRY

Mr. Chairman, there *is* a property in our office that might suit Mrs. Toothe's needs, and ours, very well indeed.

GILBERT

Not *here.*

PERRY

No; two stops up. Big house, pretty cheap, too: it's only a couple of minutes' walk from the station.

MRS. TOOTHE

Sounds very good. How many rooms?

RICHARD

How many bedrooms, you mean, don't you?

MRS. TOOTHE

Will you be quiet! (*Back to normal tone*) If the price is reasonable . . .

PERRY

Thirty-six.

MRS. TOOTHE

Twenty-eight. Yes, that will be all right. I shall look at it tomorrow. I don't want there to be too much of a gap in . . . (*Smiles*) our services.

(RICHARD *snorts*)

Look here: I've spent time, and money, and energy building up this enterprise, with a first-class clientele and . . .

RICHARD
(*Mumbled*)

All right, all right, all right . . .

MRS. TOOTHE

Well, are there any questions?

CHUCK
(Satisfied)

Fine.

GILBERT

Seems good.

MRS. TOOTHE
(To RICHARD; *none too pleasant)*

You?

RICHARD
(Again, an attempt at sarcasm)

Oh, a couple.

MRS. TOOTHE
(Impatient, but not hurried)

Well, let us have them.

CHUCK
(Chiding)

Oh, Dick . . .

RICHARD

Doesn't it seem to bother any of you . . . Christ, everybody's
going to know! Inside of two weeks it'll be all over the . . .
doesn't that *disturb* any of you?

MRS. TOOTHE

We don't advertise in the local paper.

RICHARD

There's a thing called word-of-mouth.

MRS. TOOTHE

Your wives will know if there is any danger. Believe me . . .
I know what I'm doing.

RICHARD

There's such a thing as messing on your own doorstep, isn't there?

GILBERT

That's a pretty rotten thing to say.

RICHARD

True.

GILBERT

Any other business?

CHUCK
(Guesses)

No . . .

PERRY

No . . .

RICHARD
(Heavy sarcasm)

Well, in that case, I declare the meeting closed.

MRS. TOOTHE

There is one other thing . . .

GILBERT

Mm?

PERRY

What is that?

MRS. TOOTHE

It's important that you carry on normally. You shouldn't talk about all this any more. I mean, even among yourselves.

GILBERT

We should forget it, you mean.

PERRY

Yes. We should forget it.

CHUCK

Quite right.

RICHARD
(A little quivering laugh—rage in this)
I don't quite see how we can . . . just forget it.

MRS. TOOTHE
(Wise counsel)
Oh, yes you can. One can forget. If something isn't good to
live with, or convenient, one can forget. After all, there are
things you *have* to forget if you want to live at all.

RICHARD

Yes, but . . .

MRS. TOOTHE

But you all know this. You're men of family and education.
You're not fools.

CHUCK

No; of course we're not.

PERRY

Quite right.

MRS. TOOTHE
(Rises, moves toward garden)
I think I'll go collect my ladies. *(Stops; to* RICHARD*)* One
other thing for you to remember—one thing which might
help you forget; two things: we do nobody any harm . . .

RICHARD

And the other?

MRS. TOOTHE

There's very little chance your wife will ever take a lover behind your back. *(She exits)*

GILBERT
(After a small pause)

Well, then; it's all set.

CHUCK
(Going to the bar)

Shall we drink on it?

PERRY
(Raises his glass)

Yes; here's to us.

GILBERT

To us. *(Notices* RICHARD *is just looking at his glass)* Richard? To us? To all of us?

RICHARD
(Pause, self-deprecating little laugh; raises glass)

Sure; to us.

GILBERT
(Older brother)

You'll be all *right,* old man; you will be.

CHUCK AND PERRY
(Softly)

Cheers.

RICHARD
(Little boy; something lost)

Cheers.

(The ladies start coming back in)

BERYL

I find it quite hopeless to try to grow azaleas here, and I don't
know why.

JENNY

It's the lime in the soil, I think, but you can take care of that.

BERYL

Ah, well; your thumb.

MRS. TOOTHE

Who will tend my garden? Are there local people?

CHUCK

Yes, good ones . . . but expensive.

MRS. TOOTHE

Ah, well, there will be enough . . . if everything works out.
Jenny, dear, may I use your telephone?

JENNY

Of course; let me show you.
(JENNY *and* MRS. TOOTHE *exit*)

BERYL

Well, let us ladies all have another drink, and then we must
go. It's all arranged, I understand.

CHUCK
(*Moving to the bar*)
I'll do the honors. Yes; all fixed.

PERRY

Perfect set-up.

LOUISE

Fine.

CYNTHIA

I couldn't be happier.

BERYL

Richard, no one is drinking your champagne, what a shame;
but I *will* have some of your caviar, crackers and all.

RICHARD
(Sarcasm intended)
The champagne will keep; perhaps we can use it to christen
Mrs. Toothe's new house.
(General laughter as response; sarcasm not seen)

CYNTHIA
(Giggling)

Oh, Richard; really!

(JENNY returns)

JENNY

What did I miss?

LOUISE
(Her laughter dying)
Oh, nothing; Richard said something funny.

JENNY
(Relieved)

Oh. How very nice.

*(ROGER and JACK appear in the doorway to the
garden; JACK is quite drunk, but, even so, he is exag-
gerating it)*

JACK

Hullo! Hullo! The gate-crasher is here; say hullo to the gate-
crasher. Say hullo to the gate-crasher. Say hullo!
*(They all turn, look at JACK; complete silence from
them)*

ROGER
(Giving tobacco to PERRY*)*
Here's your tobacco; I hope it's right.

JACK
Young Roger found me by the club; well, *at* it, actually; *at*
the club, and *at* the bar.

BERYL
(Cool)
That's rather evident.

JACK
Ooohhh, *honestly,* Beryl! *(Generally again)* Annnddd so,
I said to old Roger, how's the party, an' he told me, but I
thought I'd come anyway. And here I am, and all my old
friends, and isn't it wonderful.

JENNY
(Uncomfortable)
I . . . I thought you had a game, or something.

JACK
Backgammon with old Digby . . . well, old Digby died; yes
he did. Farnum was kneading away at him on the old mas-
sage table, finished up, slapped him gently on the ass and
said, "All done, Mr. Digby, sir," and he just lay there. Died
horizontal on a metal board, which is as splendid a way as
any. Got the good vod out, Richard? Got it hidden?

PERRY
(As JACK *makes for the bar)*
Go easy on the vodka, Jack.

JACK
(A dare)
Your house? Your vodka?

PERRY

No; but, still . . .

JACK

Tell you what I'll do, Perr, old thing: next time you give a
garden-type party, and I come unasked—which is the only
way I'll make it, if old Cyn has anything to say about it, eh,
kid?—*then* . . . I will go easy on the vod. O.K.?

LOUISE

Do you, uh . . . do you bring any *other* charming news
from the club with you, dear Jack?

JACK

Anything other than poor old Digby? Weeellll . . . Oh!
Yeah! They got rid of Harry Burns.

GILBERT

Got rid of him? How?

JACK

Dug back—someone did; found out it was short for Bernstein; asked him to go.

CHUCK
(*Disbelief, but not offended*)

Oh, come *on.*

JACK

True; true.

LOUISE
(*To* BERYL)

Is Monica Burns *Jewish?*

BERYL

Well; I *suppose.*

LOUISE
(Some wonder)
I never would have *thought*.

CYNTHIA
She never let *on*.

LOUISE
Can you *imagine*.

JACK
For God's sake, you'd think she was a common prostitute, or something.
(Small silence)

BERYL
(Cold)
A what?

JACK
(Wagging his head)
A prostitootsie.
(Another small silence)

CYNTHIA
I can't say that Harry and Monica look . . .

LOUISE
No, no, they don't . . .

BERYL
Funny how you can sort of know, though . . .

JACK
After the fact, you mean.

PERRY
(Wincing a little)
Threw him out of the club?

ROGER

Some people say we're *all* Jews.

JENNY
(Not offended; startled)

What?

ROGER

The ten lost tribes.

GILBERT

Some people will say anything.

ROGER

And quite a lot of us are circumcised.
(Silence, save JACK, *who laughs softly)*

RICHARD
(Short, cold)

Go to your room.

ROGER

What?

RICHARD

Go to your room!

ROGER

Why!?

JENNY

He didn't mean to say anything.

ROGER

What did I say?

RICHARD

I told you to go to your room!

ROGER
(Standing his ground)
I want to know what I said wrong!

RICHARD
(Feeling foolish; this, though, merely pushes him further)
Don't you stand there and defy *me!!*

ROGER
It's not fair! You say much worse things!

RICHARD
I am your father and I tell you to go to your room. You're not fit to associate with decent people.

JACK
(Laughing, but serious)
Oh, come on, Richard!

RICHARD
(To JACK)
SHUT YOUR MOUTH! This is my house and my son! I tell him what to do! *(To ROGER) Go on!*

ROGER
(Supplication to the rest of the group)
But it comes up all the time in the Bible.

RICHARD
So do the Ten Commandments. Do you know the Ten Commandments?

ROGER
Yes.

RICHARD
Say them.

ROGER

Now?

JENNY

Darling . . .

RICHARD
(*Wheeling on her*)
Leave me something! (*To* ROGER) Now!

ROGER

Thou shalt not kill.

RICHARD

That's one. Go on.

ROGER
(*Looks to* JENNY *for help, but there is none there*)
Thou shalt not . . . (*Falters*)

RICHARD
(*To them all*)
There; and a liar as well. Go up to your room.
        (ROGER *pauses, gives up, turns, begins going, shaking
        his head*)

JACK

The poor bastard didn't say anything.

RICHARD
(*Following* ROGER)
Are you going to go to your room, or am I going to have to
take you UP there?

JENNY
(*To* RICHARD)
Darling, let him . . . let him go out, or something. Let him

go to the club. Just . . . (*Between her teeth*) . . . get him *out* of here.

RICHARD
(*Sighs*)
Oh . . . all right. (*Exiting, calling after* ROGER) Roger? Roger?

BERYL
They do need discipline.

GILBERT
A few licks with a belt from his father never did a boy any harm.

PERRY
Mine kept a riding crop.

GILBERT
And you never resented it, did you?

PERRY
(*Can't recall*)
I . . . I guess not.

JACK
How savage you all are today. Savage . . . and strange. All embarrassed, and snapping. Have I caught you at something?

BERYL
What do you mean!

JACK
(*To audience*)
Is there something going on here?

CHUCK
Have another drink, Jack.

JENNY

Yes! Let's everybody! Perry?
(*General agreement and movement*)

JACK

(*Grabbing* JENNY *by the arm as she moves by him*)
Jenny, my darling! Why do you all hate me? Why are you
all trying to get me drunk?

JENNY
(*Artificial little laugh*)

Jack!

JACK

What's going on, Jenny?

JENNY
(*Transparently lying*)
Nothing, Jack. Nothing at all.

JACK

Do you still love me, Jenny?

JENNY
(*Soothing the little boy*)
Yes, Jack; of course.
(RICHARD *re-enters*)

JACK

Ah! Thank God! (*Rises*) Kiss and make up. (*He kisses her*)

RICHARD

I sent him out for a . . . What do you think you're doing!

JACK

I am kissing your beautiful wife.

RICHARD

Then stop it!

JACK

I *have* stopped.

RICHARD

I don't care for that sort of behavior.

JACK

Oh, come on, Richard. It might have been anyone. Hasn't Jenny been kissed before?

RICHARD

You are not to kiss her!!

JACK

What is the *matter* with all of you this evening?

BERYL

There is *nothing* the matter with us.

JACK

There is something . . . very wrong.

(MRS. TOOTHE *re-enters*)

MRS. TOOTHE

Well, my dear children, my flock, I have made the necessary calls, and I think we . . . (*Sees* JACK) Ah. (*Her eyes move from one person to another quickly*) I, uh . . . I do believe we've met before.

JENNY

(*Jumping in*)

Jack, you *do* remember Mrs. Toothe; you met her . . . oh, six-seven months ago, and . . .

JACK
(Staring at MRS. TOOTHE)
Yes; your fairy godmother.

MRS. TOOTHE
(To JACK; *very naturally)*
How nice to see you again.

JACK
How nice to see you. *(Turns away, thinking)*

MRS. TOOTHE
(To the others)
I *do* think I should be off now. It was so nice meeting you
all . . .

JACK
(Suddenly remembering)
Yes! *(Turns around, a smile of fascination)* You're English,
aren't you?

MRS. TOOTHE
(Playing it cool and natural)
British, yes.

JACK
And you lived in London . . . some, some time ago.

MRS. TOOTHE
(Hedging)
Yes, I . . . well, I *have* lived in London, but . . .

JACK
(Very pleased)
I *do* remember you, dear lady. By God, if I were *sober,* I
doubt I would. *(Laughs greatly)* Oh yes! Do I remember you!

MRS. TOOTHE
(Playing it through)
You must be mistaken. I never forget faces, and . . .

JACK
Oh, lady; I remember you well, I remember your . . . *(Another fit of laughing)* . . . your ladies, I . . . *(Looks about the room, sees the trapped and embarrassed faces, breaks into more laughter)* Oh no! No! Tell me it's not true! It is! It is true! *(More laughter)*

BERYL
I don't know what you're thinking, Jack, but I suspect that you may have had a little too much to drink, and . . .

JACK
Has Madam found herself another group of ladies? *(Laughter as he talks)* Are we operating in the suburbs now? *(Mock commiseration, laughter)* Oh, my poor Beryl! Dear Cynthia! Proud Louise! *(Sees* JENNY; *his tone now is a cross to disappointment and wonder at the future possibilities)* And oh my darling Jenny!

RICHARD
Stay away from her.

JACK
And all that . . . and all that money lying on the . . . *(Breaks into more laughter)* . . . "Someone sent it to us in the mail?" *(Laughter)* Gentlemen . . . I don't know who arranged all this; but if you guys did, you're better businessmen than I ever thought you were. *(Laughs, starts for french doors)*

MRS. TOOTHE
(Eyes narrowing)
Stop him.

PERRY

Where do you think you're going?

JACK
(Still laughing)

Hm?

PERRY

I said where do you think you're going?

JACK

Why, I thought I'd go back to the cl— *(Breaks down in laughter again)*

MRS. TOOTHE

He'll talk. *(This was a command)*

JENNY

Yes. He will.

MRS. TOOTHE
(Even more clear than before)

He'll talk.
    (PERRY grabs JACK by the arm; CHUCK steps in front of him, barring his way)

PERRY

Hold on, old friend.

CHUCK

Easy now.

JACK
(Panic and anger rising)

Let . . . Let me go. God damn it, let me . . .
    (He begins to struggle; RICHARD and GILBERT come to the aid of PERRY and CHUCK)

GILBERT

Get him!

*(They are on him, just restraining at first, but the
more* JACK *struggles, the more they are on him)*

JACK

Let me . . . Get your hands off me . . . Let! Me! God
damn it! Let! Me!

(They have him down, are on top of him)

PERRY

Hold him! Hold him down!

JACK
(Really shouting)

STOP IT! STOP IT!

MRS. TOOTHE
(On her feet, but not in a rush; a commander)
He's drunk; he'll talk. You must make him be quiet.

*(*JACK *continues to struggle, bites* CHUCK'S *hand)*

CHUCK
(In rage and reflex, strikes JACK *across the face with
the back of his hand)*
God damn you!

JACK

STOP! IT!

MRS. TOOTHE

Keep him quiet!

*(*RICHARD *grabs a pillow from the sofa and, together,
two or three of them press it over* JACK'S *face. His
shouts become muffled as they hold the pillow on
his face, stiff-armed. Finally there is silence. The
men relax a little, slowly get off their knees, unwind*

some, look at JACK's *prone, still form; they move
about a little)*

GILBERT

He's out.

RICHARD
(Grim laugh)

For a while.

MRS. TOOTHE
(Goes over, bends over JACK, *examines him for a
moment, straightens up)*
No. Not for a while. *(Begins to walk back to her chair)*

JENNY
(Pitiful; moves toward JACK)

Jack?

MRS. TOOTHE
(Cruelly casual, but serious)
Don't bother. He's dead.

GILBERT
(Offended)
What do you mean he's dead!

MRS. TOOTHE
Look for yourself. He's *dead.*

GILBERT
(Looks for himself)
Yes. He is. He's dead.
*(*JENNY *and* CYNTHIA *begin to weep, quietly;* LOUISE
turns away; the men look at one another)

BERYL
(Final; catatonic)

Well.

CHUCK

I, I don't think we did that, he . . . We didn't do that.

GILBERT

No, we were just . . .

PERRY

He must have had a heart attack.

JENNY
(Going to him)

Oh, my poor, darling Jack . . .

RICHARD

Stay away from him, Jenny.

CHUCK

What . . . what shall we do?

LOUISE
(Ordering it)

He *can't* be dead; it doesn't happen.

CYNTHIA

He would have talked! It would have been all over town.

JENNY
(Defending JACK)

Who says!?

BERYL

You said, for one.

JENNY
(Furious, and near tears)

I did not! I said . . .

MRS. TOOTHE
(Calm)

You said he would talk. You agreed he would.

GILBERT

No one meant to kill him . . .

PERRY

No, it was . . .

RICHARD
(Grim)

I think I'd better call the police, hunh?

CHUCK
(Nodding)

Yeah, yeah.

GILBERT

Yes; you'd better.

MRS. TOOTHE
(Calm, forceful)

Do you think so?

RICHARD
(Sort of disgusted)

What?

MRS. TOOTHE

Do you think you had better call the police?

RICHARD

There's a *dead* man there!

MRS. TOOTHE

I know; I can see. But what will you tell them? The police.

RICHARD

I'll, I'll tell them . . . we were having a party, and, and Jack came in, and he was drunk, and . . .

MRS. TOOTHE

And so you all smothered him?

RICHARD
(Furious)

No! That he was drunk!

BERYL

. . . he kept on drinking . . .

GILBERT

. . . and he had a heart attack.
(Pause, they look to MRS. TOOTHE)

CHUCK

No?

MRS. TOOTHE

You may call the police, if you want to. *Do* let me leave first, though. I wouldn't want to be listed among those present when the autopsy is done and they find the marks on him and the hemorrhage in the lungs. That happens when people are killed that way, you know; the lungs rupture.
(Silence)

GILBERT

Oh.
(Silence)

PERRY

I see.
(Silence)

BERYL

Well. We can't take *that* chance, can we.
(Silence. JENNY *weeps quietly)*

LOUISE
(Slowly)

No. We can't.

RICHARD
(Quietly loathing)

What do you suggest we do, then?
(They all look to MRS. TOOTHE, *save* JENNY)

MRS. TOOTHE
(To RICHARD)

I know you think I'm a monster, so . . . if I ask you a question, it won't matter much.

RICHARD
(Waiting)

Yes?

MRS. TOOTHE

What . . . what is the purpose of that deep trench you've dug near your brick wall?
(Silence)

RICHARD
(Calm response; much underneath)

I've been looking for the cesspool line.

MRS. TOOTHE

Have you found it?

RICHARD
(Still staring at her)

No.

MRS. TOOTHE
(After a pause)
Well, then. Bury him.
*(Silence. The guests look at each other, calmly,
speculatively)*

RICHARD
(Slowly)
You can't mean that.

MRS. TOOTHE
(To all the men)
Go on; bury him.

RICHARD
(Smiling a little)
No.

MRS. TOOTHE
All right, then. Call the police.
*(Silence; the men look at one another, slowly, stead-
ily. Then, as if it had all been organized, they slowly
move to work. They go to* JACK, *take him by the
legs, arms, under the head, and take him out into
the garden, disappear from our sight)*

JENNY
(After they have gone; rises, starts after them)
Jack! Richard!

MRS. TOOTHE
Jenny! Come here!
*(*BERYL *and* LOUISE *go to* JENNY, *who is helplessly,
quietly crying now, and gently bring her back to the
group. They all sit)*

JENNY
You . . . they just can't . . . do that.

MRS. TOOTHE

Hush, my dear. Hush.
> (*This is a wake and the ladies have sorrow on their faces*)

LOUISE
> (*Sincere; helpless*)

Poor *Jack*.

BERYL

Yes; poor Jack.

LOUISE

At least it wasn't . . . one of us. I mean, someone, well . . .
with a family, someone . . . regular.
> (JENNY *is quietly hysterical*)

MRS. TOOTHE

You haven't put up with death, have you, Jenny?
> (JENNY *shakes her head*)

I'm sorry to say you get used to it!

JENNY

N-never!

MRS. TOOTHE

You should have been in London in the war. You would have
learned about death . . . and violence . . . All those nights
in the shelters, with the death going on. Death and dying.
Always take the former if you can.

LOUISE
> (*Nodding at the sad truth*)

Yes.

MRS. TOOTHE

You must help your husbands. You'll have to, I think . . .
for a while. They may wake up at night; sweat; they may . . .
lose heart. You'll have to be the strong ones . . . as usual.

BERYL

Yes.

MRS. TOOTHE

I wouldn't try to make them go on as if nothing has happened. For something *has* happened . . . very much so. One of the things that *does* happen . . . one of the accommodations that have to be made. Do you see, Jenny?

JENNY

I don't know.

MRS. TOOTHE
(Sweet; gentle)

You can't go *back*. You have to make do with what is. And what is leads to what will be. You make the best as you go on. Like our looks, when we age, as we are doing, or will. Some of us have our faces lifted, I suppose, and we convince . . . some people—not as many as we'd like to—but we don't believe it ourselves, do we, Jenny?

JENNY
(A little girl at lessons)

I shouldn't think so. No.

MRS. TOOTHE

No. We do what will help, which is all we can.

JENNY
(Instructed)

Yes.

(The men come back in, subdued, clothes a little awry, hands dirty)

GILBERT

All done.

PERRY

Finished.

CHUCK

You'd never know.

RICHARD

. . . unless you had a mind.

CHUCK

Unless you knew.

RICHARD

Yes.
(*Goes to* JENNY; *in fact, all the men gravitate to their wives*)

CYNTHIA
(*Kindly*)

Would any of you like a drink? Darling?

PERRY

No; no thanks.

LOUISE

Darling?

GILBERT

Yes. A quick one.

RICHARD
(*To* JENNY; *comforting*)

You O.K.?

JENNY
(*Brave smile*)

Sure. You?

RICHARD
(Empty)

Considering.

MRS. TOOTHE

Well; you've all done very well. I think it's time I should be getting on.

BERYL

Yes; well, we all should.

GILBERT

Yes. What time are Don and Betty coming over?

LOUISE

Oh, my God! Eight o'clock. You're right, we've got . . .

CHUCK

Your husband is hungry.

BERYL

Well, all right then, I'll feed you.

MRS. TOOTHE
(To PERRY*)*

I'll call you tomorrow and come to see the house?

PERRY

Yes; fine.

RICHARD

You're all just . . . leaving?

CHUCK
(What else?)

Yes; I think we should.

PERRY

There's nothing we can do, is there?

RICHARD

(Quiet, intense)

There's a body out there; Jack.

GILBERT

It's all *right,* Richard.

PERRY

Really, Richard; it's O.K.

BERYL

Yes, it *is.*

MRS. TOOTHE

Go home, children, it's all right.

CHUCK

Yes, well, I don't know what more we can do.

LOUISE

Yes, we do have Don and Betty coming over.

CYNTHIA

Do you mean Don and Betty Grainger?

LOUISE

Yes.

PERRY

I still can't get over Harry Burns.

GILBERT

Harry Bernstein, you mean.

(The guests have gone)

MRS. TOOTHE
(*To* JENNY *and* RICHARD)

The grass will grow over; the earth will be rich, and soon—eventually—everything in the garden . . . will be as it was. You'll see.

(MRS. TOOTHE *exits, followed by* RICHARD *and* JENNY *seeing her out almost by reflex. Bare stage for a moment*)

(JACK *comes in from the garden, his clothes dirty, sod in his hair*)

JACK
(*He will speak only to the audience from now on, even when* RICHARD *and* JENNY *return; nor will they notice him, of course*)

Oh, don't get any ideas, now. I'm dead, believe me. I'm *dead*. It's amazing how dying sobers you up. Well, I certainly never thought it would be *this* way—like this; I'd imagined sliding gently from the bar stool at the club, or crashing into a truck on a curve some night, but never this. Shows you can't tell. God! Would you believe it? Mrs. Toothe, and Beryl and Cynthia and Louise? And poor Jenny? I wouldn't have; but, then, I'm rather selfish—self-concerned. *Was*. I must get *used* to that; past tense. Poor Jenny and Richard. They're the only ones I feel badly about—the guilt, and all the rest. That old Madam can take care of herself, and the others . . . who cares? But Jenny and Richard . . . that's a different matter. I *worry* for them.

(JENNY *and* RICHARD *re-enter, move about slowly.* JACK *puts a finger to his lips, to shush the audience, whether necessary or not*)

JENNY
(*Timid*)

Well.

RICHARD
(*Emptied*)

Yes.

JENNY
(Trying to be conversational)
Where did you send Roger?

RICHARD
To the club. To swim.

JENNY
(Genuine)
That was nice of you.

RICHARD
Stupid taking it out on him.

JENNY
Yes. *(Pause)* I think we'd better clean up—all the glasses and everything.

RICHARD
All right.

JACK
(Watches them for a moment; back to the audience)
Here's the *awful* irony of it.

JENNY
(Remembering)
We're to say . . . nothing.

RICHARD
What will happen? He'll have just . . . disappeared?

JENNY
Yes; I guess so.

RICHARD
Roger *brought* him here.

JENNY

Yes, but we'll say Jack just stayed for a little, and then went on.

RICHARD

They'll ask?

JENNY

Someone will; someone's bound to—insurance people, some· body.

RICHARD

We must make a story.

JENNY

Yes. I'll talk to the others.

RICHARD

All right.

JENNY
(So sincere; explaining so much)
Darling . . . I do *love* you.

RICHARD
(Timid)
Yes; and I love you.

JACK

The irony; I was going to tell you the irony. Remember I said I'd made my will over, left it all to Richard and Jenny? Well, it was true; I wasn't kidding. Three and a half million; every penny, and my house here, *and* in Nassau. It's all theirs.

JENNY

Let's put the glasses on the tray here.

JACK

Problem now is, they'll have to wait. If I've just . . . vanished . . . disappeared from the face of the earth, it'll be seven years until I can be declared officially dead. And there'll *be* an investigation; you can be sure of that. I hope they make it stick—the story they tell. I imagine they will.

RICHARD

What shall I do with the caviar?

JENNY

Give it here; I'll cover it and put it in the fridge.

JACK

But seven years; that's a very long time. So much can happen. With all they're doing, in seven years their lives can be ruined. They have so much to live with. (*To* RICHARD *and* JENNY) You've got to be strong! You've got to hold on!

JENNY

Darling?

RICHARD

Mmm?

JENNY

I was thinking . . . that house Mrs. Toothe is taking.

RICHARD

What about it?

JENNY

I think it ought to be planted nicely, flowers and shrubs and all. Make it look like it's really lived in. It mustn't look like it's been let go. It might draw suspicion. You notice things like that.

RICHARD

Yes; you do.

JENNY

Gardens that have been let go. If people let them go, you know there's something wrong in the house.

RICHARD

Yes.

JENNY

I think it should be well planted and taken care of; kept up. I think it should look like all the others. Don't you think so?

RICHARD
(Straight)

Yes; I think you're right.

JACK

Well . . . I think they'll make it.

CURTAIN

EDWARD ALBEE

Edward Albee was born in 1928, and began writing plays thirty years later. His previous plays are, in order of composition, THE ZOO STORY (1958); THE DEATH OF BESSIE SMITH (1959); THE SANDBOX (1959); THE AMERICAN DREAM (1960); WHO'S AFRAID OF VIRGINIA WOOLF? (1961–1962); THE BALLAD OF THE SAD CAFÉ, *adapted from Carson McCullers' novella* (1963); TINY ALICE (1964); MALCOLM, *adapted from James Purdy's novel* (1965); *and* A DELICATE BALANCE (1966).